The

Project

Management

Playbook

A Comprehensive Guide to Mastering Your Role as a Project Manager and Beyond

Contents

The Project Management Playbook

Introduction

Welcome to "The Project Management Playbook." This book has been created to help you navigate the world of project management. You may be a seasoned professional who wishes to improve your skills or even if you are a project manager in training moving from business analyst to project manager, this playbook will help you. It is designed to be your companion on your journey to becoming a seasoned project manager or getting you started on your path to successful project execution.

Purpose of the Book

I started creating this book when I noticed that many new project managers required additional support within our work environment. While I was always happy to answer questions, I realised the importance of creating a resource that could always be available for new project managers even if I was not available at the time. So, you will find that the essence of this book is to help you demystify the art and science of managing projects. Considering the world of project management, one thing is certain is that change is constant. That means businesses evolve constantly and project

The Project Management Playbook

management is necessary to hold many initiatives together. Eventually when the right project management processes are employed by project managers then improvements can be seen in the delivery of projects. This playbook equips you with the knowledge, tools, and insights to manage projects efficiently, handle stakeholders adeptly, and lead your teams to success.

What's Inside

Throughout the pages of this book, you will have an inside look into the principles and practices that I have personally used to launch successful projects with my team. You will get insights into the principles and practices that underpin this success. From mastering the art of project planning to learning the art of internal and external stakeholder management, each chapter provides clear and concise guidance, augmented by real-world examples, case studies, and insightful tips and tricks.

The Project Management Playbook

Infographics are interspersed throughout the book to provide visual representations of complex concepts, helping to reinforce learning and make the information more digestible. The diverse range of topics covered will empower you to approach projects with confidence, anticipate and mitigate risks effectively, and develop solutions that align with organisational goals.

PROJECT MANAGEMENT PLAYBOOK

Who Can Benefit?

The Project Management Playbook

1. Young & Budding Business Analysts: Gain a solid understanding of what project management entails and build a foundation for a successful career.
2. Project Management Professionals: Refine your existing knowledge and skills and stay updated on the latest trends and best practices in the field.
3. Business Leaders & Entrepreneurs: Learn how to optimise project outcomes and drive organisational success through effective project management.

Navigating the Playbook

Each chapter is structured to facilitate easy navigation, allowing you to progress sequentially or jump to specific sections as needed. Practical examples and real-life scenarios are provided to illustrate the applicability of theoretical concepts, and reflection points are included to encourage critical thinking and self-assessment.

As you embark on this journey through "The Project Management Playbook," I am confident you will find valuable insights, acquire new skills and be more adept at leading projects to their successful completion. With that in mind, it's time to start your journey through the world of project management. Let's get started!

Chapter 1: What is Project Management?

CHAPTER 1

Project management is often used in many business contexts, yet it may be a good idea to get back to the basics of what makes project management different to other business areas such as business analysis. Project management is the core of many projects across different industries and business areas.

Perhaps you may have seen this in action where ideas get converted into tangible business outcomes despite many challenges and variables at play.

The Project Management Playbook

Here's a tangible example to illustrate this point. A software development company looks to create a new software product to help small businesses manage their financial health. A project manager is assigned to oversee the development of this software product. They may start with a project plan highlighting objective, time required, and budgets. The project manager is responsible for ensuring that each team plays their role effectively and delivers their piece of the puzzle on time and on budget. Meanwhile, a business analyst's role is different in that they identify business problems and needs and define solutions. For this project, the business analyst would conduct market research to understand the needs of small businesses, determine what features the software should have, and document the software requirements.

Attribute	Project Manager	Business Analyst

Objective	Oversee the development and execution of the project.	Identify business problems and needs and define solutions.
Main Responsibilities	Develop project plans including objectives, times, and budgets. Monitor the progress of each team and ensure deliverables are on time and on budget.	Conduct market research to understand user needs and determine software features. Document software requirements.
Focus Area	Execution, Monitoring, and Control of project tasks.	Analysis of business needs and solution definition.

Outcome	Ensure successful delivery of the project within scope, time, and cost constraints.	Ensure the final product meets the identified business needs and solves the defined problems.
Tools	Project Management Software, Risk Management Tools, Scheduling Tools.	Data Modelling Tools, Requirement Management Tools, Survey/Questionnaire.
Key Skill Sets	Leadership, Time Management, Risk Management, Scheduling, Budgeting.	Requirement Analysis, Market Research, Solution Assessment, Documentation.
Result	Successful completion and delivery of the	A well-defined and documented solution meeting

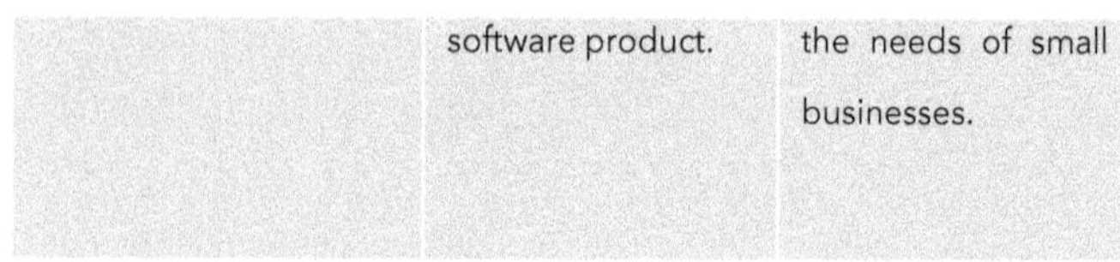

As indicated by the table above, there are differences in each role of project management and business analysis. Yet in today's dynamic and rapidly evolving business world, the need for great business analysis and proficient project management is critical. In my previous book, The Business Analyst's Playbook, I highlighted in detail the role of a business analyst and this book will highlight the next step on the career ladder, in the form of project management. So, to get started let's look at projects versus project management.

1.1 Projects vs Project Management

A project is a temporary endeavour that results in a unique product or service. There is a clear beginning and end which is different from the daily operations of a business. This means that each project could be considered unique and non-repetitive. The aim always being to complete a goal identified as a business need or problem. Examples of these projects are those that meet a need from a consumer or fills a service gap in the market.

Ultimately it will improve the business operations and essential to the company bottom line. While that defines a project, there is a unique difference between a project and the management of that project. It is not simply about a project manager overseeing tasks and ensuring they are completed. It is more than that, it is about using the knowledge, skills and tools learned to meet and exceed the objectives set. The project manager is therefore a conductor of many elements such as scope, time, cost, quality and risk. The project manager conducts each aspect so that value is delivered to the business stakeholders. Ultimately, this requires a balance of planning, flexibility, innovation and creativity on the part of the project manager.

The following table illustrates the difference between projects and project management

Attribute	Projects	Project Management
Definition	A temporary endeavour to create a unique product or service with a clear beginning and end.	The application of knowledge, skills, and tools to meet and exceed the project's objectives.
Nature	Unique and non-repetitive.	Systematic, requires a balance of planning, flexibility, innovation, and creativity.
Focus	Creating a unique outcome, usually a product or service, to fulfil a specific need or solve a specific problem.	Overseeing and conducting various elements like scope, time, cost, quality, and risk to ensure the project's success.

Outcome	A completed product or service that meets a consumer need or fills a service gap in the market.	Delivery of value to business stakeholders through successful conduct and completion of the project.
Role in Business	Improves business operations and contributes to the company's bottom line.	Ensures that the project meets and exceeds its objectives, delivering optimal value to the business.
Essential Skills	Understanding of the market need, clarity in scope and objectives.	Leadership, strategic planning, risk management, flexibility, and knowledge of project management tools and techniques.

Here is a good summary showing the key differences between projects and project management.

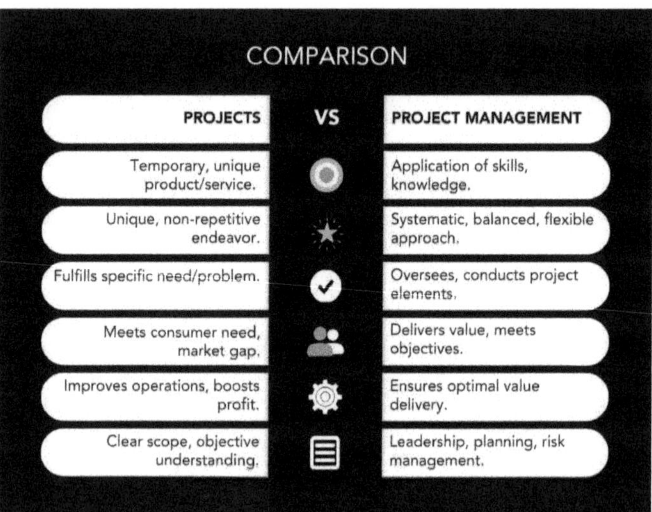

1.2 The Evolution of Project Management

A long time prior to the formal discipline of project management, history shows the achievement of amazing projects. One example that springs to mind is the pyramids of Egypt or the Great Wall of China.

And while it might seem strange to think that these monuments required project management, but if you think about it, it required the ability to conceptualise, plan and create these wonders of the world. Even so, it was not called project management at the time. It was not until the 20th century where project management became a distinct discipline as technology erupted and new industries emerged. The need for project management was due to the complex projects needed to build a technologically advanced society that we know today. While this book is in no way a history book, I've decided to briefly highlight some important milestones in the birth of project management to what we know it today.

Evolution of Project Management

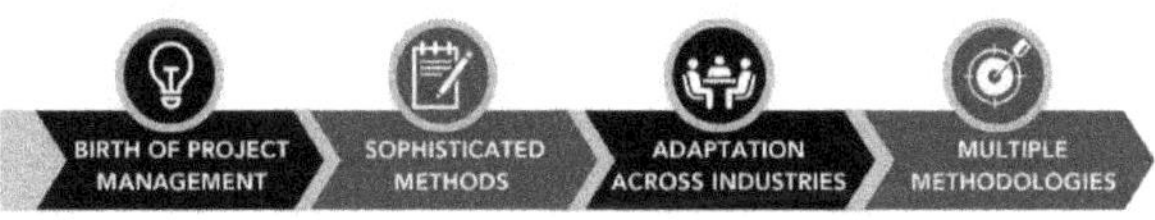

The 1900s: Gantt Charts and The Birth of Project Management

During this time, the focus was on improving efficiency and helping people and technology be more productive. One visionary was Henry Gantt who created processes and tools for project scheduling. Therefore, the Gantt chart was born and continues to be used today to measure timelines and monitor project progress. Here is an example of the modern-day version of the Gantt chart.

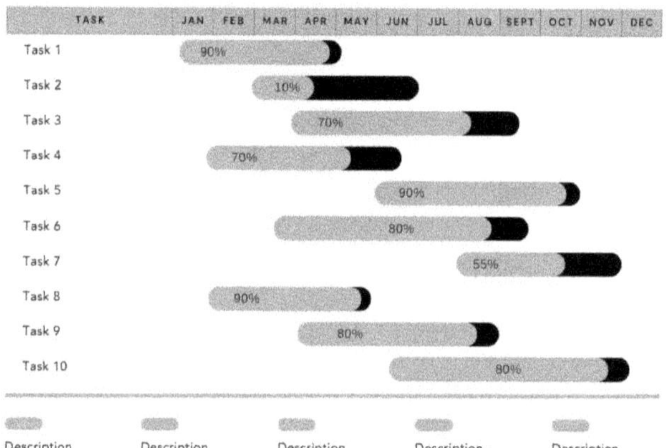

The Mid-20th Century: Rise of Sophisticated Methodologies

Once the Gantt chart had become prominent, there was need for more advanced methods too such as the Critical Path Method (CPM) as well as the Program Evaluation and Review Technique (PERT). These methods allowed for better analysis of project tasks and project managers could quickly identify important tasks and then allocate resources effectively. It made the execution of projects more streamlined.

Method	Description
Gantt Chart	Visualizes project schedule.
CPM	Identifies critical tasks, allocates resources.
PERT	Analyses tasks, streamlines execution.

The Diversification Era: Adaptation across Industries

Over time, the essence of project management infiltrated many domains of business from IT to healthcare. It changed and evolved to meet the unique needs of each industry. This era marked universal applicability of project management approaches.

The Contemporary Age: Multiple Methodologies

Today project management is filled with many methodologies. For example, traditional Waterfall models coexist with Agile and Lean methodologies. This offers many approaches to navigate the demands of various projects. The Waterfall model, with its sequential phases, offers clarity and structure. On the other hand, Agile methodologies embrace flexibility and responsiveness.

Year	Event	Description
The 1900s	Birth of Project Management	Focus on improving efficiency with the creation of Gantt Charts by Henry Gantt for project scheduling, measuring timelines, and monitoring project progress.
Mid-20th Century	Rise of Sophisticated Methods	Introduction of advanced methods like Critical Path Method (CPM) and Program Evaluation and Review Technique (PERT) for better task analysis and streamlined project execution.
Diversification Era	Adaptation across Industries	Project management principles infiltrated various business domains, evolving to meet the unique needs of

		each industry, marking the universal applicability of project management approaches.
The Contemporary Age	Multiple Methodologies	Coexistence of multiple methodologies like Waterfall, Agile, and Lean to navigate the demands of various projects, balancing structure with flexibility and responsiveness.

1.3 Importance of Project Management

You have seen how project management has evolved over time and it has become the lifeblood of most organisations today. Here is a summary of how valuable project management can be to your organisation. Also included are examples highlighting each point.

Aspect	Description	Example
Achieving Organisational Objectives	It can mould organisational goals into realities through planning and execution. Also, ensures there is alignment with strategic visions and creation of value.	A pharmaceutical company developing a ground-breaking drug requires proficient project management to align diverse research teams, manage trials, and

		ensure regulatory compliance.
Optimising Resources	Acts as the steward of resources ensuring optimal utilisation and minimising wastage.	In constructing a skyscraper, meticulous resource allocation and scheduling are crucial to prevent delays and cost overruns, ensuring every resource is aligned and synchronised.

Managing Risks	Identifies and mitigates risks inherent in any project. Anticipates potential roadblocks and formulates contingency plans to safeguard project trajectory.	Robust project management strategies in IT projects are crucial for managing uncertainties and rapid changes, ensuring uninterrupted progress.
Successful Delivery of Projects	Coordinates and integrates diverse elements crucial for the successful delivery of projects.	The launch of the Mars Rover mission by NASA was not just a triumph of technology but also of meticulous project management, ensuring inter-departmental coordination and meeting timelines.

| **Ensuring Stakeholder Satisfaction** | Aligns stakeholder expectations and delivers outcomes that meet or exceed these expectations. Addresses stakeholder needs and incorporates feedback. | Whether launching a new product line or implementing a new IT system, effective project management is crucial in enhancing stakeholder satisfaction and value. |

1.4 Characteristics of a Project

As noted, projects are different from standard day to day operations of a business. As such, there are characteristics that make a project what it truly is. Let's consider these characteristics which were highlighted earlier. Now, I will go into further detail.

It is temporary

Projects have a marked beginning and end point. That means it is finite. This can be helpful in the early stages of a project as the objectives and scope can be clearly defined. This ensures projects go ahead right through to its completion. Usually, at the end of a project timeline, it can be a delivery and outcome.

It is unique

Projects are unique in that at the outset it requires a tailored approach, specialised solutions and individualised specific plans and execution. While projects may have similarities, it cannot be the same. That's the reason why in the planning phase, a project must be analysed considering its unique needs, stakeholder expectations and challenges as well as solutions. And it should also have adaptive management when it reaches the execution stage always aligning with the goals and stakeholder requirements.

It progressively expands

Since projects are dynamic, as they progress more information becomes available. This requires a need for refined plans, schedules, and strategies. This is a good thing as it ensures that you as the project manager remain open and responsive to new insights, altering requirements and sudden developments. This has always will link back to the project objectives and business expectations.

It has a life cycle

The life cycle of a project is four-fold, namely the initiation phase, planning phase, execution phase and the closing phase. Each phase is characterised by specific outcomes. As a project manager, recognizing and understanding each stage of the life cycle will help you successfully manage projects.

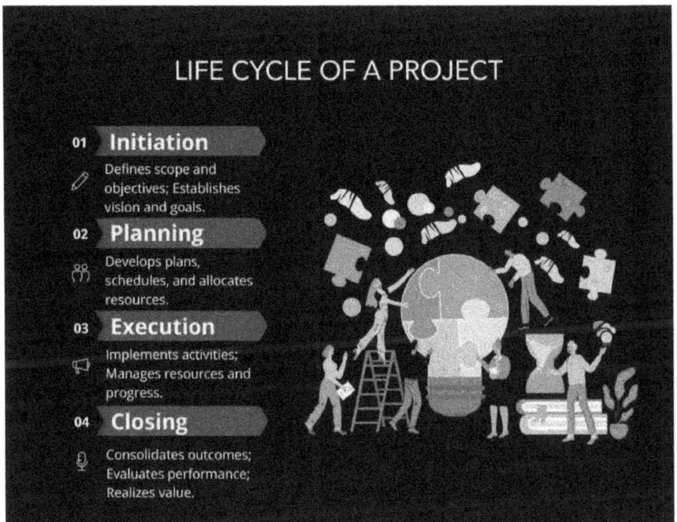

It creates a dynamic environment

Overall, the characteristics of the project and the interactions makes a dynamic environment which creates synergy. Therefore, even though each project has inherent uncertainties and is complex, it can still deliver value and achieve its goals. As a project manager, it helps to always keep in mind the different characteristics of a project and use this to your advantage.

1.5 The Triple Constraint

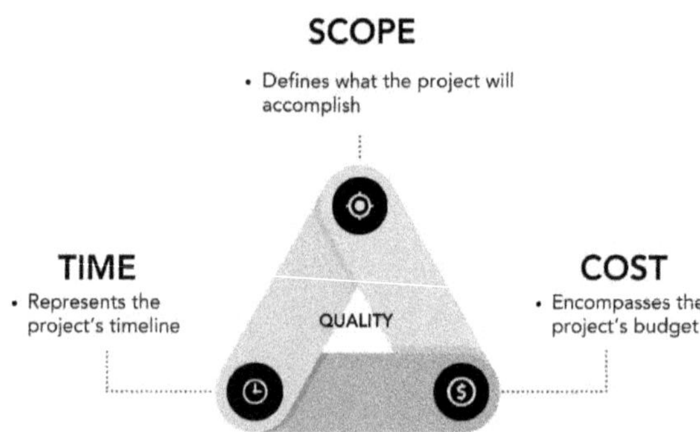

The quality of any project is impacted by the constraints of Scope, Time, and Cost. Collectively, this is known as The Triple Constraint in project management. Let's consider this in more detail below including how it impacts on the quality of a project.

Component	Description	Impact on Quality
Scope	Defines what the project will accomplish, outlining the objectives, deliverables, features, and	Understanding the interrelation is crucial: altering scope may require adjustments in time and cost to maintain quality. Expanding scope may require more time and

	functions.	costs.
Time	Represents the project's timeline, including the deadlines for completing various tasks and the project.	Reducing time may require a narrower scope or increased costs to expedite tasks, impacting the overall quality of the project.
Cost	Encompasses the project's budget, reflecting the financial resources allocated for executing the project.	Alterations in cost, driven by changes in scope or time, may impact the available resources and thus the final quality of the project.

1.6 Key Components of Project Management

The key components that guide a project are Project Scope, Schedule, Budget, Quality, Risk Management, and Stakeholder Management. Let's look at each of these processes in more detail.

Aspect	Description	Example
Project Scope	Outlines what needs to be accomplished, defining objectives, deliverables, and boundaries. Provides a clear roadmap for what the project will achieve, acting as the project's backbone.	A new software development project has a defined scope, including objectives like improved user experience, clear deliverables like a feature set, and boundaries like software functionalities.

Schedule	Details the timeline for the project, outlining when tasks should be completed, and milestones reached. Pivotal for tracking progress and ensuring timely delivery of the project.	The software development project has a detailed schedule, marking the completion dates for each feature development and milestones like alpha and beta releases.
Budget	Represents the financial blueprint, detailing costs, and resource allocation. Critical for maintaining financial control and ensuring the project remains within financial constraints.	The project has a budget allocated for each phase, considering resources, labour, and unforeseen expenses, ensuring financial viability.

Quality	Ensures the project's output meets required standards and stakeholder expectations. Focuses on the reliability, durability, and performance of the product or service.	Quality management in the project ensures each feature meets the defined standards and user expectations, undergoing rigorous testing phases.
Risk Management	Involves identifying, assessing, and mitigating risks that could potentially derail the project. Crucial for navigating uncertainties and ensuring project stability.	Risks like software bugs and delays are identified early in the project, with mitigation strategies like buffer times and additional resources in place.

Stakeholder Management	Involves managing the expectations and concerns of individuals or groups with an interest in the project. Crucial for maintaining harmony and achieving project success by addressing the concerns of involved parties.	Regular updates and feedback sessions are held with stakeholders like end-users and investors to address concerns and align expectations.

1.7 Frequently Asked Questions

What exactly is project management?

Project management is the practice of initiating, planning, executing, controlling, and closing a project to achieve specific goals within a set timeframe, while considering constraints like scope, quality, time, and budget.

How is a project different from everyday operations?

A project is a temporary endeavour with a specific start and finish, aiming to achieve a unique goal. In contrast, everyday operations are ongoing, repetitive activities that sustain an organisation's business functions.

What are the primary components of project management?

The primary components include the project's scope, schedule, resources, quality, risks, communications, stakeholders, and costs.

Why is project management important for businesses?

It ensures that projects are completed on time, within budget, and meet the defined objectives. It also helps in optimizing resources, managing risks, and satisfying stakeholders.

Who is a project manager, and what's their role?

A project manager is an individual responsible for leading a project from its inception to completion. They plan, execute, and close projects, ensuring they meet specific success criteria.

Are there specific methodologies in project management?

Yes, there are various methodologies like Waterfall, Agile, Scrum, Lean, and PRINCE2, among others. The choice of methodology depends on the project's nature, industry, and specific requirements.

What's the difference between objectives and deliverables in a project?

Objectives define the specific goals or outcomes the project aims to achieve. Deliverables, on the other hand, are tangible or intangible outputs produced because of the project.

How do project managers handle risks?

Risk management involves identifying potential risks, assessing their impact and probability, and then developing strategies to mitigate or respond to them.

Why is stakeholder management vital in project management?

Stakeholders can influence or be influenced by the project. Effectively managing stakeholders ensures their expectations are aligned, potential issues are addressed, and the project garners necessary support.

Is project management relevant only for large projects or enterprises?

No, project management is beneficial for projects of all sizes and across industries. Even small projects can benefit from structured planning, resource allocation, and risk management.

1.8 Chapter Summary

In Chapter 1, you learned about Project Management from core components to the historical evolution. You explored project management showing how it is a multidimensional process that optimises resources, manages risk, and delivers value to stakeholders. Let's summarise everything you learned in chapter 1. Feel free to check off each item once you have completed it.

Section	Action Point
Introduction to Basics	Review fundamental definitions and concepts of project and project management.
Historical Journey	Trace and reflect on the evolution of project management from ancient to contemporary methodologies.
Project Characteristics	Study and understand the distinctive traits of a project including its temporariness and uniqueness.
Triple Constraints	Learn and comprehend the management of Scope, Time, and

	Cost, and their impact on project quality.
Core Components	Explore and understand the importance and integration of Scope, Schedule, Budget, Quality, Risk Management, and Stakeholder Management.
Reflect and Review	Reflect on the real-world applicability of each component and characteristic and review each section for thorough understanding.

In the next chapter, you will get clarity on the foundations of project management, and I will provide you with essential frameworks so you can swiftly improve your skills as a project manager and deliver successful projects.

Chapter 2: The Foundations of Project Management

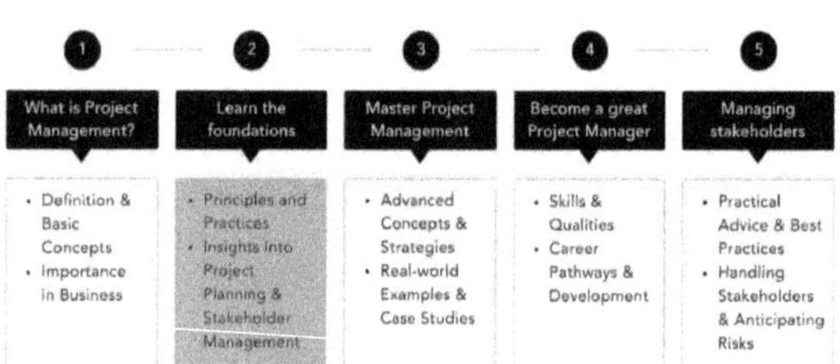

In this chapter, you will learn more about the foundations of project management. The information included will also highlight the PMBOK. PMBOK stands for the Project Management Body of Knowledge. It is a set of standard terminology and guidelines for project management. It is published by the Project Management Institute (PMI). The PMBOK outlines a framework and best practices that project managers can use to manage projects successfully.

In the context of the PMBOK, the five process groups are:

- Initiating
- Planning
- Executing
- Monitoring and Controlling
- Closing

These process groups organise the different phases of managing a project from start to finish.

The PMBOK also divides project management into ten knowledge areas. Each of the knowledge areas represent a field of practice with its processes, tools, and techniques. These knowledge areas are important in understanding and applying the appropriate methodologies in project management. This ensures that projects are completed efficiently and effectively.

Understanding and applying the concepts from the PMBOK can significantly help new and seasoned project managers in their project management journey. For the simple fact that it provides structured approaches and best practices to navigate the complexities of managing projects. So, let's start by looking at the five process groups in more detail.

2.1 The Five Process Groups

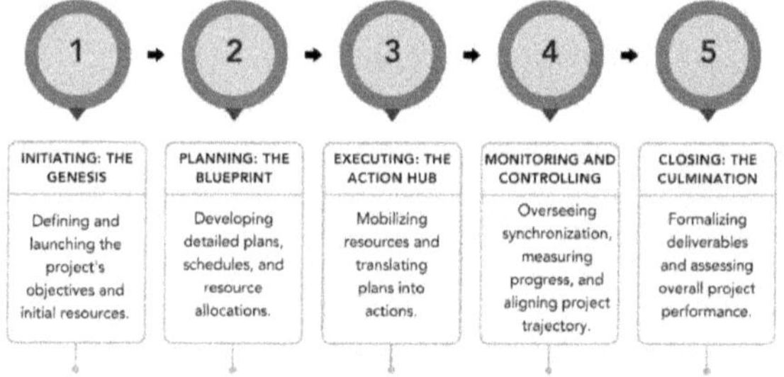

The Process Groups serve a vital role in project management, offering guidance to project managers. They help attain specific objectives, steering any project from early stages to completion. Let's consider each group in more detail.

The Project Management Playbook

Process Group	Description	Action Point
Initiating: The Genesis	The project is born, defined at a macro level, and set in motion. It involves crystallising the project's objectives, pinpointing stakeholders, and earmarking initial resources.	Review and define project objectives
Planning: The Blueprint	The project begins to take shape through meticulous planning, carving finer details, weaving schedules, delineating resources, and mapping out elements such as scope, risk, and quality.	Develop detailed plans and schedules

Executing: The Action Hub	This is where plans are translated into actions, resources are mobilised, teams are synchronised, and tasks are conducted, morphing visions into reality.	Mobilise and synchronise resources
Monitoring and Controlling: The Balancing Act	Operating concurrently with execution, this phase oversees the synchronisation between plans and actions, measures progress, and institutes controls to align the project trajectory with the established plan.	Monitor progress and institute controls

Closing: The Culmination	This marks the completion of the project lifecycle, where deliverables are formalised, handed over, and the overall performance and outcomes of the project are assessed and documented.	Assess and document project performance

Now that you have clarity on the Five Process Groups, you can see the vital stages that projects must go through to ensure a successful project. Additionally, the five process groups are not enough, you must get acquainted with the ten knowledge areas which I will highlight in detail for you next.

2.2 Mastering the Ten Knowledge Areas

The PMBOK specifies ten distinct Knowledge Areas as shown below.

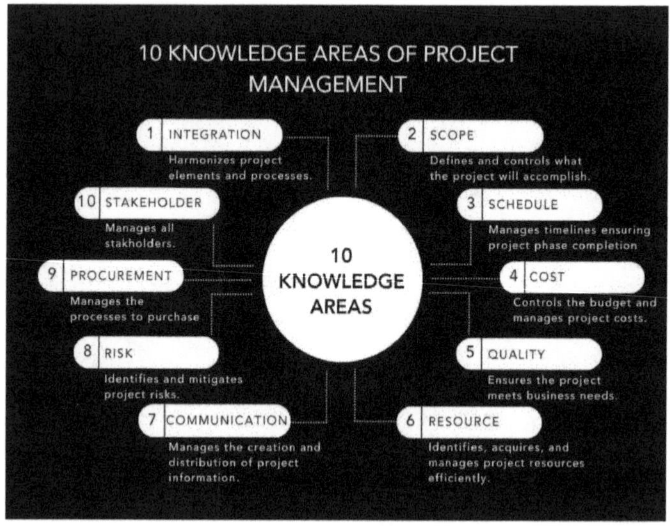

In this section, you will gain more insight into each knowledge area and how you can leverage it for your projects.

Knowledge Area	Description	Case Study

Integration	Harmonizes various elements and processes, ensuring seamless blending of project elements.	Coordinating various departments to work together on a construction project.
Scope	Sets project boundaries and ensures alignment with project's objectives.	Clearly defining the deliverables for a software development project to avoid scope creep.
Schedule	Manages processes for project's timely completion.	Developing a detailed timeline to ensure a marketing campaign is launched on schedule.
Cost	Plans, controls, and manages the project's budget.	Monitoring expenses and adjusting budgets to avoid overruns in an R&D project.

Quality	Establishes and adheres to quality policies, objectives, and responsibilities.	Implementing quality assurance processes to meet the quality standards in a manufacturing project.
Resource	Identifies, acquires, and manages resources optimally.	Allocating team members and equipment effectively for an event organisation project.
Communication	Handles the creation, collection, distribution, storage, retrieval, and disposition of project information.	Ensuring clear and timely communication to keep stakeholders informed during a system integration project.
Risk	Involves planning, identifying, analysing, and	Identifying and mitigating potential risks in a new product

	responding to project risks.	development project.
Procurement	Manages the processes to purchase or acquire necessary products, services, or results.	Negotiating and finalising contracts with suppliers for a logistics project.
Stakeholder	Identifies and manages entities that could impact or be impacted by the project.	Addressing concerns and expectations of different stakeholders in a community development project.

2.3 Application and Real-world Scenarios

Most of this chapter has been showcasing theoretical frameworks that are popular and useful in project management. However, the real value for a project manager is when the principles and frameworks can be applied to real world scenarios. For example, in construction projects, the use of civil engineering, compliance and architectural design must be coordinated seamlessly to bring the project to fruition.

Another example is the healthcare sector where quality is non-negotiable since it could result in devastating effects if not adhered to. Therefore, project management must ensure robust processes that also align with medical standards.

Finally in the IT sector, where it is quite fast paced, it can be seen and applied in software development projects where there must be a clear definition at the outset of objectives and deliverables. If not, there will be a case of scope creep (which we will discuss in more detail later in this book). When project management principles are used effectively it supports IT teams to deliver software to stakeholders when expected and at the right quality standard.

Considering these real-world applications, let's look more in depth at the latter example in IT where I use the 5 process groups and link them to the knowledge areas you learned.

The Project Management Playbook

Process Group	Knowledge Areas	Activity
1. Initiating	Integration Management	Defined project start points and initial project objectives.
	Stakeholder Management	Identified internal teams, the client, and end-users as key stakeholders.
2. Planning	Scope Management	Outlined software functionality and features; established project boundaries.
	Schedule Management	Developed a timeline, setting milestones for each

		development phase.
	Cost Management	Estimated costs for resources, labour, and technologies; allocated the budget.
	Quality Management	Set standards for coding, user interface design, and user experience.
	Resource Management	Allocated development, design, and testing resources.
	Communication Management	Established communication plans for status updates and feedback.
	Risk Management	Identified potential risks including scope creep and technology-related issues.

	Procurement Management	Detailed procurement plans for third-party services and technologies.
3. Executing	Integration Management	Implemented planned activities, ensuring coherence with project objectives.
	Resource Management	Mobilised allocated resources.
	Communication Management	Facilitated information flow among stakeholders.
4. Monitoring and controlling	Schedule Management	Tracked progress against planned milestones; made adjustments as needed.
	Cost Management	Monitored spending, ensuring alignment with the budget.

	Quality Management	Checked deliverables against set standards.
	Risk Management	Assessed and mitigated newly identified risks.
5. Closing	Integration Management	Completed and concluded all project components, gaining client acceptance.
	Stakeholder Management	Gathered and evaluated feedback from stakeholders.
	Procurement Management	Finalised and closed all procurement contracts.

That's a process you can follow in your projects too, leveraging the principles set out in the PMBOK guide and applying them as you start taking on bigger projects along the way. However, there is still more useful information to learn as you progress through this book and after I summarise this chapter, I will take you through effective tips and tricks to take your project management skills up a notch.

2.4 Frequently Asked Questions

What are the foundational principles of project management?

The foundations encompass defining clear objectives, careful planning, effective communication, proactive risk management, stakeholder engagement, and continuous monitoring and evaluation.

How do project objectives influence the project's direction?

Clearly defined objectives provide a roadmap for the entire project. They help ensure that every action taken aligns with the project's intended outcomes and provides a benchmark against which success can be measured.

Why is planning often considered the most critical phase in project management?

Planning sets the stage for all subsequent project activities. A comprehensive plan outlines the scope, timeline, resources, and budget, ensuring that everyone knows their roles and the project's direction.

What role does communication play in the foundational stages of a project?

Effective communication ensures that all stakeholders are informed, aligned, and actively engaged. It also aids in preventing misunderstandings, managing expectations, and fostering collaboration.

How can I identify and engage key stakeholders effectively?

Start by mapping out individuals or groups that can influence or are affected by the project. Then, determine their interests and influence levels to prioritize engagement activities. Regular communication, feedback loops, and involvement in decision-making are key.

Are there standardized tools or techniques for foundational project management?

Yes, tools like Work Breakdown Structures (WBS), Gantt charts, and risk matrices are commonly used. The choice of tools often depends on the project's nature and complexity.

Why is risk management considered a foundational element?

Every project carries inherent uncertainties. Proactively identifying, assessing, and planning for risks ensures that the project is better prepared to handle challenges and deviations.

The Project Management Playbook

How is the scope of a project determined and managed?

A: Scope is determined by defining clear objectives, deliverables, and requirements. It's managed using a scope statement, scope baseline, and regular reviews to avoid scope creep (unplanned changes or additions).

Can the foundations of project management be adjusted once a project has started?

While the foundational principles remain consistent, specific elements like scope, resources, or timelines might require adjustments due to unforeseen changes. However, any adjustment should be well-considered, communicated, and documented.

How do foundational project management practices differ across industries?

While the core principles remain the same, industry-specific nuances, regulations, and best practices can influence how these foundations are applied. For instance, software projects might prioritise agile methodologies, while construction projects might focus on physical resource management.

2.5 Chapter Summary

In Chapter 2, you went further into the fundamentals of Project Management. You explored the five process groups and knowledge areas as shown by PMBOK. You learned how a project manager can significantly impact project outcomes. In doing so, I hope it has highlighted the value of mastering the ten knowledge areas and applying them. Below is a structured summary of the content covered in Chapter 2. Once you have completed each section, feel free to check off each item.

Section	Action Point
Five Process Groups	Review the five process groups and consider how you can apply this to your next or current project.
Ten Knowledge Areas	Reflect on the ten knowledge areas and determine which area needs work on your projects.
Application and Real-World Scenarios	Look at the scenarios presented and learn from the steps.
Reflect and Review	Reflect on the real-world applicability of each component and characteristic and review each section for thorough

understanding.

In the upcoming chapter, you will explore how to master the art of project management. I will show you the exact skills and attributes required to become an effective project manager. I will also show you how to use the tools and strategies to take your skills to the next level.

Chapter 3: Mastering the Art of Project Management

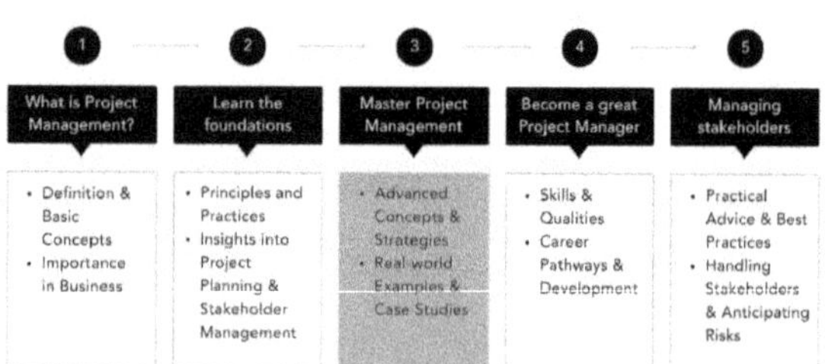

Mastering project management is akin to mastering an art form, requiring a fine balance of technical knowledge, interpersonal skills, foresight, and adaptability. In this chapter, we explore the essential skills and attributes needed to become a successful project manager and delve into the nuanced arts of planning, risk management, and leadership within project management.

3.1 Skills and Attributes of a Successful Project Manager

The Project Manager wears many hats in any organisation, and perhaps this is true within your company too. The project manager may have to be a leader, communicator, mediator and even strategist when the occasion arises. Due to this broad range of requirements, project managers must have or gain the necessary skills to ensure they fulfil their role effectively. Therefore, in this section, I'll breakdown the skills and attributes you need to be a successful project manager.

Skill	Description	Strategies
1. Technical Proficiency	Understanding the technical dimensions to oversee development, discern nuances, and make informed decisions. Overseeing a complex software development project, discerning technical nuances, and	<ul><li>Regular learning.</li><li>Staying updated on industry advancements.</li><li>Seeking mentorship.</li></ul>

	solving related issues.	
2. Communication Skills	Ensuring precise articulation and reception of ideas, expectations, and feedback amongst stakeholders and team members. Managing communications in a diverse team, ensuring clear and transparent information exchange between team members and stakeholders.	• Regular training in interpersonal and communication skills. • Active listening. • Clarifying intentions.
3. Problem-Solving and Critical Thinking	Addressing unforeseen challenges during a marketing campaign by employing structured problem-solving frameworks.	• Employing structured problem-solving frameworks. • Encouraging diverse perspectives.

4. Leadership	Nurturing a collaborative culture and directing the project trajectory towards its goals. Leading a team at the organisation through a high-stakes project by inspiring through vision and values.	• Leadership workshops and coaching. • Developing emotional intelligence. • Providing guidance for the team.
5. Time Management	Managing and optimising time are crucial to adhere to schedules and guarantee the punctual delivery of milestones. Employing time management tools to ensure punctual delivery of milestones in a logistics project.	• Employing time management tools. • Setting realistic goals. • Allocating sufficient buffers for unexpected delays.
6. Risk Management	Proactive anticipation, identification, and	• Regular risk management

Skills	neutralisation of risks. Developing contingency plans for potential risks in a construction project.	training. • Scenario planning.
7. Customer-centric mindset	Maintaining open lines of communication and iterating based on customer insights in a product development project.	• Regular review of customer feedback. • Ongoing learning in customer relationship management.

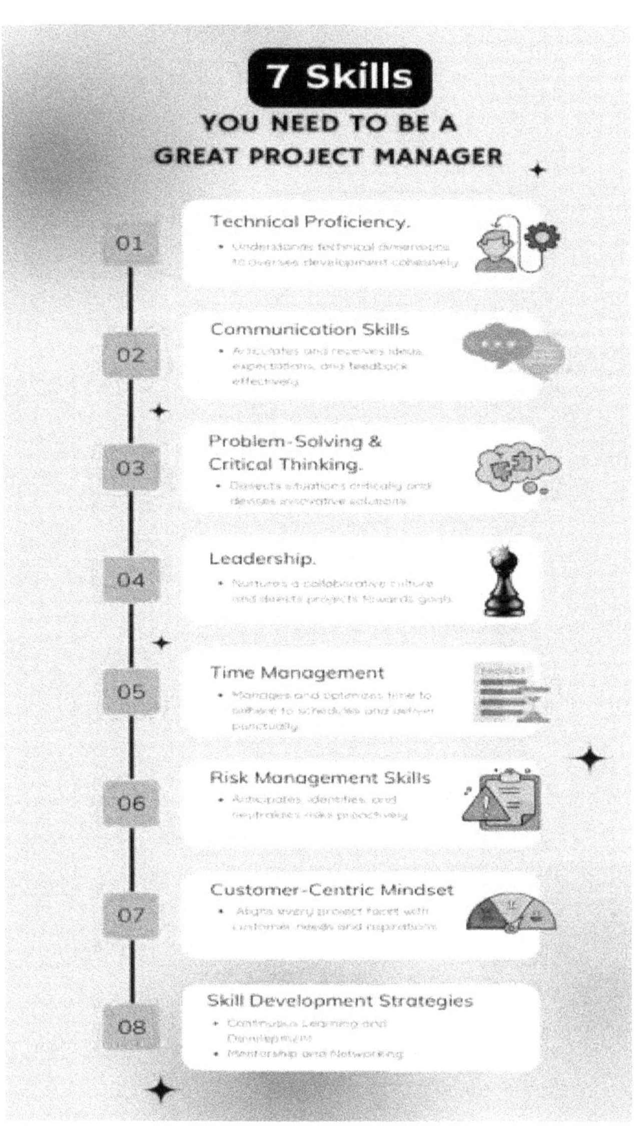

The Project Management Playbook

Practical Skill Development Strategies

Additionally, I have highlighted practical ways to develop your skills below:

- Continuous learning and development, mentorship and networking, real-world application, and feedback integration are crucial for refining competencies.
- Applying learned concepts to real-world scenarios in various projects and improving approaches based on feedback.
- Pursue certifications as offered by the Project Management Institute (PMI)
- Attend workshops and read extensively,
- Seek guidance by expanding your professional network
- Apply learned concepts, and value constructive feedback.

The infographic below will summarise everything you need to know about the skills needed to be a great project manager.

3.2 Strategies and Insights for Optimised Project Blueprinting

The framework of any project is its plan. This plan includes details, timelines, resources and sets the tone for what the project will become. In this way, effective planning synchronises clarity, detail, and flexibility making sure that the initial idea matches the desired result at the end. For that there are six focus areas that will ensure that you create the perfect project blueprint at the outset. Here are the six strategies to use in your projects.

The Project Management Playbook

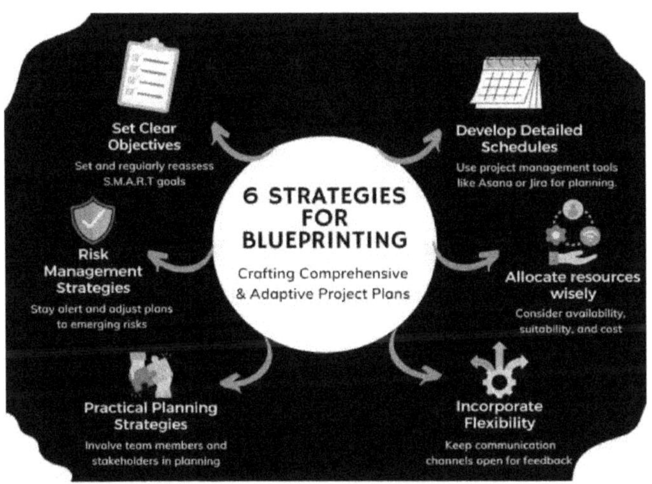

Strategy	Description
1. Setting Clear Objectives	• Do this through strategic alignment. This ensures that every goal for the project matches organisations strategies and stakeholder needs. • Set S.M.A.R.T Goals which are simply objectives. These objectives must be • Specific, Measurable,

	Achievable, Relevant, and Time-bound. In this it will offer clarity and direction. • Always reassess the objectives set. Regularly revisit and refine so that you can confirm the goals are still valid.
2. Developing Detailed Schedules	• Take a granular approach to tasks. This means breaking down the project into small tasks that are achievable. This will make it clear for you and your team. It also makes the tasks manageable. • Allocate sufficient time so this means setting realistic timeframes for tasks. Always keep in mind potential obstacles and add some buffer time too. • Set milestones which will serve to help you monitor progress. As you monitor progress, you may see a need for adjustments. These

changes will help keep you on track to meet the project goals.

- There are many planning tools in the form of project management software which will help create, adjust and monitor schedules. Examples include Asana, Jira or Monday.

3. Allocating Resources Wisely

- Assess the resources needed. Consider availability, suitability, and cost.
- When allocating resources, do so mindfully. This means you should not overcommit resources. You can do this by planning and researching in the early stages of the project.
- Finally, monitor continuously. When you regularly review how resources are used, you can quickly spot adjustments

	needed.
4. Incorporating Flexibility:	• Create plans that are adaptive. This means that your plans should have the capacity to evolve and accommodate changes and uncertainties along the way. • Use scenario planning to your advantage. You can do this by anticipating potential changes and challenges. In this way, you can create your contingency plans for various scenarios. • Don't hesitate to open the channels for feedback. Be open to the insights offered up from team members and stakeholders. This will make your project stronger.
5. Proactive Risk Mitigation	• Create a system to regularly identify the risks and disruptions that may occur during the project. • Develop strategies

	beforehand to minimise the impact of the risks identified. • Be alert to the project environment for emerging risks. Adjust the project accordingly.
6. Practical Planning Strategies	• Be collaborative as you plan. This means getting your team members and the stakeholders involved. It's a good idea to use diverse insights and this will create collective ownership. • Be consistent with reviews. Do this by regularly revisiting the plan, adjusting the details as needed. • Aim for clear documentation. This might seem tedious but can be helpful in terms of clarity and transparency for all involved in the project.

Planning might seem like extensive work, and it is. That said, it is one of the most important parts of your project. It ensures that you are working on the correct aspects of business objectives and that all team members and stakeholders are involved. This can bring clarity to the road ahead. And while planning is quite important, do not underestimate the power of risk management as well. Let's consider how you can effectively manage the risks in your project.

3.3 Strategies for Effective Risk Management

Since many projects are uncertain, and there can be unforeseen circumstances, you need a risk management process to mitigate against uncertainty and challenges. There are many strategies you can leverage which will help you anticipate and navigate potential project pitfalls. Below, I elaborate on six key strategies and approaches that ensure the resilience and adaptability of your projects.

Area	Description

1. Identifying Risks Early	• Take a comprehensive risk analysis approach. You should leverage tools like SWOT and risk breakdown structures to spot issues early on. • Get stakeholder input. Don't hesitate to involve diverse groups in risk identification. • Stay continuously vigilant by updating the risk register accordingly.
2. Prioritising Risks	• Create a risk assessment matrix. This helps you evaluate and prioritise risks based on likelihood and impact. • Perform a qualitative & quantitative analysis. By doing so, you can analyse and rank risks accurately. • Focus your resource allocation on high-priority risks.
3. Developing Mitigation	• Be proactive when planning.

Strategies	Create strategies to prevent and reduce risk impact.
	• Develop contingencies which help prepare plans for unavoidable risks
	• Remember to stress testing your mitigation strategies.
4. Monitoring Risks Continuously	• Take time to do regular risk audits. In this way you can adapt new strategies in response to evolving risks.
	• Look out for key risk indicators. As you define and monitor these indicators, you improve your reaction time.
	• Be open to feedback so that you can get it timeously.
5. Risk Response Strategies	• You can avoid, transfer, mitigate or accept risks.
	• Avoid by modifying plans to eliminate or protect objectives from risks.
	• Transfer risk impact to a third party.
	• Mitigate risk probability.

	• Accept the existence of risks without special control efforts.
6. Enhanced Risk Communication	• Be a transparent communicator by keeping communication lines open about risks. • Keep proper risk documents. That means it should be detailed and regularly updated. Include the risks, statuses, and response. • Ensure that stakeholders know what is going on with risk priorities, statuses, and mitigation.

While you may not have to integrate all these strategies to every project. Keeping them in mind, will help you mitigate risks should they arise. It will help you ensure the project stays on track despite the uncertainty and challenges that come up.

3.4 Navigating Team Dynamics and Embracing Leadership in Project Management

Teams can get things done when diverse individuals work together for a common goal. This is also true for a project management team. Leadership skills are therefore essential for a project manager. This section will look at the team dynamics and using leadership to create a conducive environment for projects to thrive. The strategies will help you to ensure everyone who is involved in the project does what needs to be done, and this positively impacts everyone on the team.

Strategy	Description
1. Cultivating a Conducive Team Environment	• Ensure that the environment created is one of trust and mutual respect. Try and make sure every voice is valued. Embrace different

	perspectives.
	● Be open in your communication style. Encourage all to be transparent, address concerns as they arise. Set clear expectations and give feedback timeously.
	● Use recognition and rewards as a positive reinforcement approach. It will ensure team members are motivated to accomplish project goals.
2. Empowering and Enabling Project Members	● Make sure the groups have the tools and knowledge needed to ensure a smooth project delivery.
	● Encourage a sense of ownership, don't be shy to delegate authority when needed. This will also help support better decision making in the group.
	● Be an advocate for ongoing learning and development. Create resources for this learning to take place.

3. Leveraging Diverse Strengths and Skills	• Different group members have unique strengths, understand, and use these effectively. Great assessments include Myers-brigg or Strengthsfinder. • Since projects will occur cross-functionally, aim to promote collaboration with different business units. • Be culturally intelligent knowing that cultural diversity helps tap into more unique perspectives.
4. Exemplary Leadership and Influence	• Model excellence in your daily engagement. Model the behaviour you hope to see. • Always be clearly communicating the project's vision and bring a sense of clarity. • Be a flexible and

	resilient leader. Adapt your leadership style accordingly.
5. Managing Team Dynamics	• There will often be conflicts during projects and various stakeholders. It helps to proactively address conflicts. This will ensure your project is more collaborative. • You could consider a team building activity if it is a long-term project. Alternatively, a kick off ice-breaker meeting may also help. • Create how you will give feedback. It's a good idea to have a robust feedback loop. This brings clarity and guidance to all.
6. Evaluating and Enhancing Team Performance	• Show key performance indicators for the project regularly. This helps team members

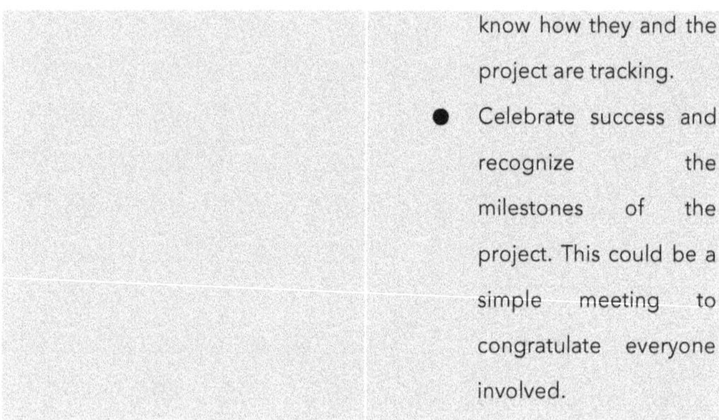

> know how they and the project are tracking.
> - Celebrate success and recognize the milestones of the project. This could be a simple meeting to congratulate everyone involved.

While project management does not seem like it would have a leadership aspect to it, it is a highly valuable area to keep your eye on. Bringing leadership to the project will enhance your ability to deliver on the project to the organisation.

3.5 Frequently Asked Questions

What distinguishes a good project manager from a masterful one?

The Project Management Playbook

While both might be proficient in technical skills and methodologies, a masterful project manager blends these with soft skills, adaptability, foresight, and an intuitive understanding of team dynamics and stakeholder needs.

Why are soft skills emphasized in mastering project management?

Technical skills lay the groundwork, but soft skills like communication, leadership, and emotional intelligence are pivotal in navigating challenges, fostering team cohesion, and ensuring stakeholder alignment.

How can I develop a proactive approach to project management?

Cultivate a habit of anticipating potential challenges, seeking feedback regularly, and staying updated with industry trends. Regularly review and adapt your strategies to cater to evolving project needs.

In what ways can intuition play a role in project management?

Intuition, built from experience and insights, can guide decisions where data might be lacking, helping in situations like conflict resolution, risk assessment, or when making judgment calls.

How can a project manager foster a positive team culture?

By promoting open communication, recognising, and rewarding achievements, creating an inclusive environment, and leading by example in terms of work ethic and attitude.

What role does continuous learning play in mastering project management?

The field of project management is always evolving. Continuous learning ensures you stay updated with the latest methodologies, tools, and best practices, allowing you to deliver projects more efficiently.

How can I better manage stakeholder expectations as I master project management?

Regular communication, setting clear expectations from the start, and involving stakeholders in key decisions can help manage and align their expectations with the project's progress.

Can mastering the art of project management be industry-specific?

While the core artistry is universally applicable, nuances and best practices might differ by industry. A masterful project manager will adapt their approach based on the project's nature and industry context.

How important is feedback in the journey to mastery?

Feedback is invaluable. It offers perspectives that you might overlook, helping refine strategies, improve team dynamics, and elevate the overall project execution quality.

What's the relationship between risk management and mastering project management?

Mastering project management involves a deep understanding of risk - not just identifying it, but proactively finding innovative solutions, ensuring the project remains on track despite unforeseen challenges.

The Project Management Playbook

3.6 Chapter Summary

In Chapter 3, you learned to master the art of project management. You explored the necessary skills and attributes required to become a star project manager. Additionally, I showed you the tools that project managers use daily to achieve their business objects. In doing so, I hope it gives you more motivation to keep learning and growing your project management skills now and in the future. Below is a summary of the content covered in Chapter 3. Once you have completed each section, check them off and keep them in mind as you go through the next chapters.

Section	Action Point
Skills and Attributes of a Project Manager	Review the key skills and attributes of a project manager. Think about your current skills, and what you can improve to be a better project manager.
Strategies and Insights for Optimised Project Blueprinting	Review your last project and consider how you can optimise the planning phase.

Strategies for Effective Risk Management	What strategies will you employ to manage the risks associated with your current projects?
Navigating Team Dynamics	Look at your team dynamics and find areas where it could be more enhanced and aim to act on this area.
Reflect and Review	Reflect on the real-world applicability of each component and characteristic and review each section for thorough understanding.

In the next chapter, I have prepared the most important resources you can leverage to become a good project manager through education and continuous learning. In addition, you will learn from a case study in the IT industry.

Chapter 4: Path to Becoming a Good Project Manager

You have certainly travelled through the various stages of understanding project management, learning the foundations, mastering key strategies and now it's time to kick it up a notch. Perhaps you are at the phase where you have mastered the basics and want to give yourself an edge within your field, then it's time to start looking at improving your skills through education, certifications, and other real-world experiences. In this chapter, you will learn how to gain the education, certification and experience needed to make you a great project manager who can work in diverse domains. I will start by showing you the education and certification pathways.

4.1 Educational and Certification Pathways

Embarking on the journey to become a skilled project manager involves delving into relevant educational and certification pathways, each serving as a beacon, illuminating the path to enhanced knowledge, credibility, and mastery. Each pathway holds its significance, bestowing unique benefits, and shaping the contour of one's professional development.

Pathway	Description
1. PMP (Project Management	● Global hallmark of

Professional)	• excellence in project management • Requires fulfilment of education, experience, and examination requirements • Conveys leadership, strategic, and business management skills • Enhances credibility and opens doors to new opportunities
2. CAPM (Certified Associate in Project Management)	• Entry-level certification for newcomers to project management • Validates understanding of elementary knowledge, processes, and terminology of project management • Demonstrates commitment and foundational understanding of project management principles • Ideal for aspiring project managers seeking to gain a competitive edge
3. Continuous Learning	• Engage in workshops, seminars, specialised

	courses to gain insights into specialised domains and emerging trends ● Contributes to nuanced proficiency and adaptable expertise ● Allows for specialised skill development in niche areas

Each of the avenues highlighted are important and beneficial. These pathways offer professional credibility and provide in-depth knowledge and insights into project management as a field. In this way, it can help facilitate your career advancement and you may eventually increase your earning potential. Finally, if you have always wanted to explore new skills in other project management areas, you can use this as a stepping stone. I have also created a breakdown of the requirements for each certification.

PMP	CAPM

1. Education Background:

- Secondary degree (high school diploma, associate degree, or global equivalent) OR
- Four-year degree (bachelor's degree or global equivalent) OR
- Post Grad degree from an accredited program. This could be a bachelor's degree, master's, or the global equivalent.

2. Project Management Experience:

- Secondary degree holders: 7,500 hours leading and directing projects.
- Four-year degree holders: 4,500 hours leading and directing projects.

1. Education Background:

- Secondary diploma (high school diploma / global equivalent).

2. And one of the following:

- 1,500 hours of project experience OR
- 23 hours of project management education completed by the time of the exam.

3. Project Management Education:

- 35 contact hours of formal education.

4. Exam:

- A multiple-choice, computer-based exam, consisting of 180 questions to be answered in 230 minutes.

4. Exam:

- A multiple-choice, computer-based exam, consisting of 150 questions to be answered in 3 hours.

Please review the above and apply to the project management institute (PMI) for these certifications once you meet the criteria.

The Project Management Playbook

4.2 Continuous Learning

Within the fluid and perpetually transforming realm of project management, the necessity to remain abreast of innovations and incessantly refine one's competencies cannot be overstated. Continuous learning and meticulous professional development are the linchpins of sustaining relevance and enhancing efficacy in project execution, acting as the conduits for attaining new heights of proficiency and wisdom in the discipline.

Learning Option	Description of Training	Examples
1. Regular Training and Workshops:	Acquiring Advanced Knowledge Skills advancement Understanding change	Engaging in a webinar on emerging project management tools can enlighten

		project managers about new techniques, helping them stay ahead of industry advancements.
2. Networking	Getting to know diverse perspectives Broadening horizons Fostering collaboration	Attending project management conferences Attending local community meetings. Joining professional meetups.
3. Experiential Learning	Improving project implementation. Enhance decision making. Refine project blueprinting.	Analysing the execution of projects. Reflecting on project setbacks and reviewing what could be improved.
4. Feedback and Mentorship	Get guidance Support regarding challenges Enhance professional growth.	Constructive feedback from a senior colleague. Mentorship from experienced

The impact of your professional development and project success can be vastly improved through education and ongoing learning. This type of learning will support you as the project management landscape grows and changes. Additionally, you will enhance your skill set for the better. As you relentlessly improve your knowledge and skills you become a more proficient project manager. This enables you to handle more complex projects. As a project manager, you can also improve your decision-making skills based on what you learn, your experiences and this will help you make more strategic decisions. Finally, your approach to problem solving takes on a new style since you have a balanced view with more diverse perspectives. This can spark innovation and help you solve more advanced problems. Now, it's time to turn your attention to a real-world case study. This will give you more practical knowledge applying everything you have learned so far.

4.3 Case Study: John's Success in Managing IT Projects

John is a Senior Project Manager at an IT company that makes software. He started as a Software Developer after finishing his studies in Computer Science and moved up to managing projects due to his excellent organisational and people skills. He also got a PMP certification to learn more about managing projects. John uses creative problem solving to help him think out of the box and this helps him solve project challenges. John also uses a flexible work method, which means he can quickly adapt to changes and deliver results fast.

These are a few of the challenges John has experienced:

- Technological Changes: Keeping up with new technology and integrating it into projects was a constant struggle.
- Managing Different Stakeholders: It was tough for John to manage the different needs and expectations of all project stakeholders and keep everyone informed about the project progress.

The Project Management Playbook

However, John was able to overcome these challenges by improving his process, he educated himself on updated technology changes and applied that learning. In addition, he learned how to manage different stakeholders. He created a robust communication framework to ensure he touched base with all stakeholders. This example gives insights into how John was able to adapt to new situations, improve his communication style well with different people involved in a project, and continually look for ways to improve work processes and outcomes.

4.4 Frequently Asked Questions

What are the fundamental skills a good project manager should possess?

A good project manager should have a blend of technical, organisational, and soft skills, including project planning, risk management, leadership, communication, and problem-solving abilities.

How important is formal education in becoming a good project manager?

While formal education can provide foundational knowledge and a structured approach, hands-on experience, continuous learning, and adaptability are equally, if not more, essential in the dynamic realm of project management.

How can I improve my communication skills as a project manager?

Attend communication workshops, practice active listening, seek feedback, and immerse yourself in environments that require varied communication styles, like team meetings, stakeholder interactions, and public speaking events.

Is it essential to have industry-specific knowledge to manage projects effectively in that sector?

While a general understanding of project management can be applied across industries, having industry-specific knowledge can significantly aid in understanding nuances, stakeholder expectations, and potential challenges more intimately.

How do I handle difficult stakeholders or team members?

Open communication, empathy, and understanding their concerns are key. It's essential to find common ground, set clear expectations, and sometimes seek mediation or third-party interventions if necessary.

What role does networking play in becoming a good project manager?

The Project Management Playbook

Networking can provide insights into best practices, offer mentorship opportunities, and expose you to diverse project scenarios, helping you broaden your perspective and toolkit.

Is certification crucial for becoming a good project manager?
While certification can validate your skills and knowledge, becoming a good project manager is more about practical application, continuous learning, and the ability to lead and adapt in varied situations.

How can I cultivate a proactive approach to challenges in projects?
Regularly review potential risks, encourage open communication in your team to identify early signs of issues, and always have contingency plans in place.

How do I balance between adhering to a plan and being adaptable in project management?
A good project manager understands the importance of a structured plan while also recognizing that flexibility is essential. Regular reviews, stakeholder feedback, and understanding the project's ultimate objectives can help strike this balance.

What are the hallmarks of a good project manager in today's digital age?
Along with traditional project management skills, familiarity with digital tools, understanding of remote team dynamics, and adaptability to fast-paced changes are becoming increasingly significant.

4.5 Chapter Summary

In Chapter 4, you received clarity on the path to becoming a good project manager. You learned about the two key qualifications known as **Certified Associate in Project Management (CAPM)** and **Project Management Professional (PMP)** that will help you advance as a project manager. In addition, I showed you how to get these qualifications. Aside from this, you now have a clear roadmap to keep learning as a project manager. In doing so, I hope it shows you a pathway to achieving project management excellence. Below is a summary of the content covered in Chapter 4. Once you have completed each section, feel free check them off and make notes where necessary.

Section	Action Point
Education and Certifications	Review the main education and certifications required to be a great project manager. Think about your current knowledge and qualifications, and what you need to take the certifications.
Continuous Learning	Review any conferences, meetups or professional meetings in your area, and

	book time in your calendar to attend.
Case Study	What strategies will you employ from the case study to grow your project management career?
Reflect and Review	Reflect on the real-world applicability of each component and characteristic and review each section for thorough understanding.

In the next chapter, I share the most valuable tips and tricks to efficiently handle your projects (big or small) as well as managing your stakeholders. You will learn three key ideas about communicating effectively, managing your time and budgets accordingly.

Chapter 5: Tips & Tricks to Efficiently Handle Projects & Stakeholders

Over the last few chapters, I have shown you the foundations needed to master the skills of being a good project manager. You have learned the key ingredients needed to make any project successful. I often like to think of managing a project like baking a cake. And while it might be simplified thinking of it in this way, it might be helpful. To bake a great cake, you need the right ingredients, in the right quantities and mixed in the correct proportions. With that said, let's consider a few key ingredients to handle projects and stakeholders successfully:

- Being clear and effective in your communication. This is all about making sure everyone knows what's happening, why it's happening, and what's expected of them.

- Know the timelines and stick to them as much as possible. It's a reality that projects have deadlines, and I will share tips on how to make sure everything gets done on time without last-minute hiccups.

- Be clear on the budget for your project. No one wants to run out of money before a project is finished. You will look at ways to budget smartly and make sure funds are spent wisely.

- Building Strong Relationships. A project isn't just tasks and timelines. At the end of the day, It's about people. You will learn about how to work well with everyone involved, from team members to managers to clients.

By the end of this chapter, you'll have a clearer understanding of these 'recipe' elements and how to mix them together for a successful project. Let's start by shaping how you communicate.

5.1 The Art of Communication

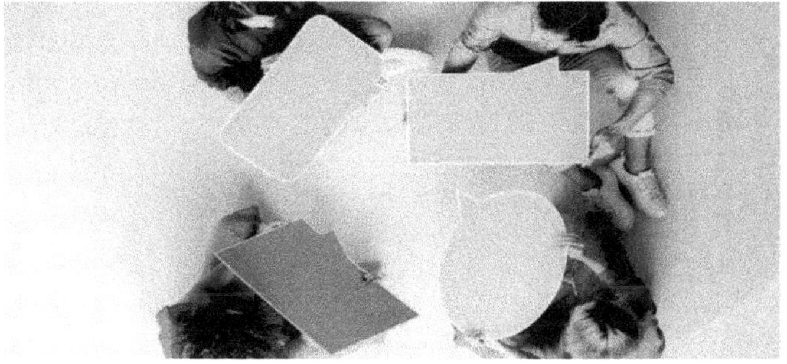

Ever chat with someone and leave thinking you're both on the same page, only to find out later that you completely misunderstood each other? It's a bit like that game "telephone" we played as kids. One person whispers something to the next, and by the time the message gets to the end of the line, it's entirely different from what was first said. This can be funny in a game, but in the world of project management, it's a recipe for disaster.

Communication, you see, is the heartbeat of any project. It's how we make sure everyone knows the game plan, understands their role, and feels confident about the journey ahead. Without clear communication, it's like trying to build a puzzle with half the pieces missing. Frustrating, right?

That's the biggest challenge for project managers. Let me give you an example to illustrate. A team member, let's call him Tom, once shared with me that he assumed everyone was on the same page about a project deadline. He thought he had clearly communicated that a report was due on Friday. But half the team understood it as "start working on it by Friday." Well, it came as a shock to everyone that it was not the case. By the time Friday rolled around, they were miles apart in terms of progress. This caused unnecessary tension, overtime, and a rushed job. Not ideal.

So, how do you avoid these pitfalls? How do you ensure that your messages are received as intended? Let's go over this step by step.

Bridging Understanding

Communication isn't just about talking; it's about making sure what you're saying is understood. Think of it as a bridge between what's in your head and what needs to be in someone else's.

Aligning Objectives

Imagine a rowing team where everyone has a different idea of which direction to row. It would be chaos, right? Similarly, in a project, everyone needs to row in the same direction. We'll discuss ways to ensure everyone knows and agrees on the end goal.

The Project Management Playbook

Ensuring Transparency

When team members feel left in the dark, they can't perform at their best. It's like trying to find your way through a room with the lights off. You will explore tools and strategies to keep everyone informed, so there are no nasty surprises or hidden obstacles.

By the end of this section, you'll have a toolkit of strategies and insights to make sure communication in your projects is clear, effective, and inclusive. No more "telephone" misunderstandings.

Aspect	Description	Examples
Clear and Concise	Convey information in a straightforward and succinct manner, avoiding ambiguities and complexities.	• Instead of "The project deadline might perhaps be tentatively around the end of next month", say "The project deadline is at the end of next month". • Use bullet points or visuals in presentations to

		break down complex topics.
Regular Updates	Keep everyone informed about project progress, changes, and developments through regular updates and meetings.	• Weekly status emails updating stakeholders on project milestones achieved. • Monthly team meetings to review tasks completed and set objectives for the upcoming month.
Active Listening	Attentively listen to others' views, concerns, and feedback, fostering an inclusive and collaborative environment.	• In a meeting, after a colleague has spoken: "What I'm hearing is that you did not get sufficient feedback. Did I capture that right?"

		• Asking open-ended questions like "Can you tell me more about that?" to encourage deeper discussions.
Feedback Loop	Encourage and value feedback from team members and stakeholders, using it constructively to enhance project outcomes.	• After presenting a project plan, ask: "What are your thoughts on this approach? Are there areas of improvement?" • Using tools like surveys or feedback forms at the end of a project phase, and then reviewing and implementing useful feedback in the next phase.

Included you will find a detailed infographic with actionable points for your reference.

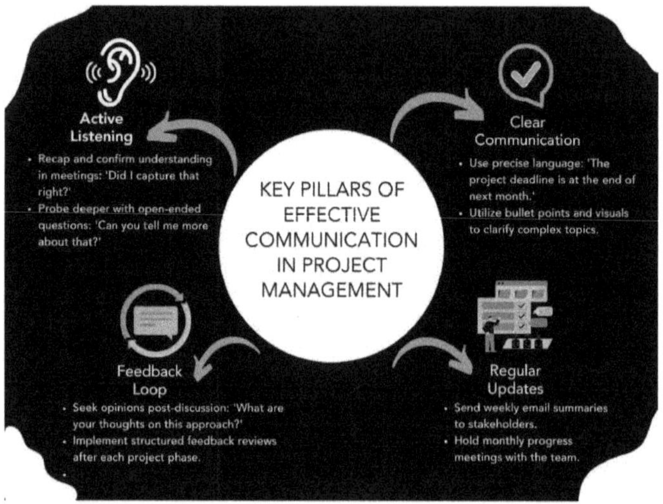

5.2 Time Management

Ever felt like there just aren't enough hours in the day? Like you're racing against the clock, and it always seems to be winning? You're not alone. A team member once quipped to me, "Time is the one thing they're not making any more of!" And she's right. While we can't create more hours in a day, we sure can make the most of the ones we've got.

Time management isn't just about counting minutes or hours; it's about using it to your advantage. It's taking that finite resource and making sure every minute is pushing your project forward. Think of it like this: if our project's journey is a road trip, then time management is our GPS, guiding us through the most efficient route. A recent example of lack of time management almost derailed my project. My team spent copious amounts of time perfecting a specific task, so they had little time to update the rest of the tasks. They ended up rushing through the subsequent stages, leading to errors and a final product that wasn't up to par. A painful lesson learned.

So, how can you dodge these time-traps? How do you ensure every minute counts? Let's embark on that journey together.

It's no good having a fantastic product if it's delivered late. I will discuss how to set realistic timelines and stick to them, ensuring your projects cross the finish line and with time to spare. You will get clarity on the following key areas:

Optimising Productivity

Time is like money. It's not about how much you have, but how you use it. I will show you tried and tested methods to maximise productivity, making sure every moment spent gives you the best outcome.

Avoiding Unnecessary Delays

Delays happen, but many can be anticipated and avoided with a bit of foresight. You will learn techniques to see them coming and strategies to steer clear.

By the end of this section, you'll be armed with techniques to not just manage, but master time. No longer will the clock be your enemy. In fact, it'll be your trusty sidekick, marching in step with you towards project success.

Aspect	Description	Examples
Prioritisation	Clearly define and rank tasks based on their importance and urgency, focusing on high-priority activities.	Using the Eisenhower Box to categorise tasks as urgent/important, not urgent/important, urgent/not important, and neither. Starting the day with

		three "Most Important Tasks" and ensuring they are completed before addressing lesser priorities.
Scheduling	Develop realistic schedules, allocating sufficient time for each task and considering potential disruptions.	Using tools like Google Calendar or Trello to map out daily and weekly tasks, accounting for breaks and buffer times. Blocking out "deep work" periods in the calendar where interruptions are minimised, ensuring focused task completion.

Time Tracking	Monitor time spent on tasks diligently, identifying areas for improvement and ensuring adherence to schedules.	Utilising time tracking apps like Toggl or Time Doctor to monitor how long individual tasks take.
		Conducting weekly reviews to evaluate if tasks are taking longer than expected and adjusting future planning accordingly.
Avoiding Procrastination	Cultivate discipline and motivation, addressing tasks promptly and avoiding unnecessary delays.	Applying the "two-minute rule": If it takes less than two minutes, do it now.
		Breaking tasks into smaller steps to make

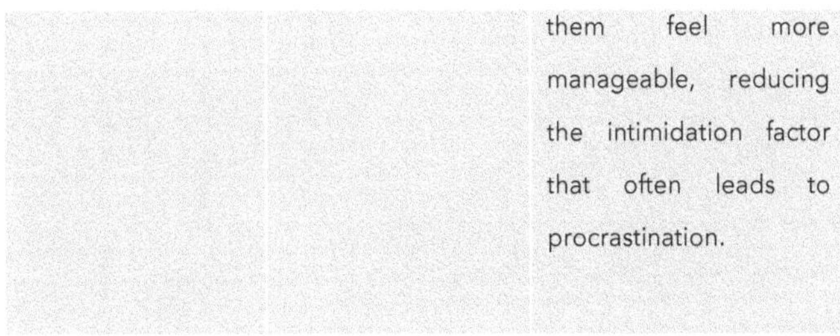

Here is a summary of the tools you can employ to better manage your time.

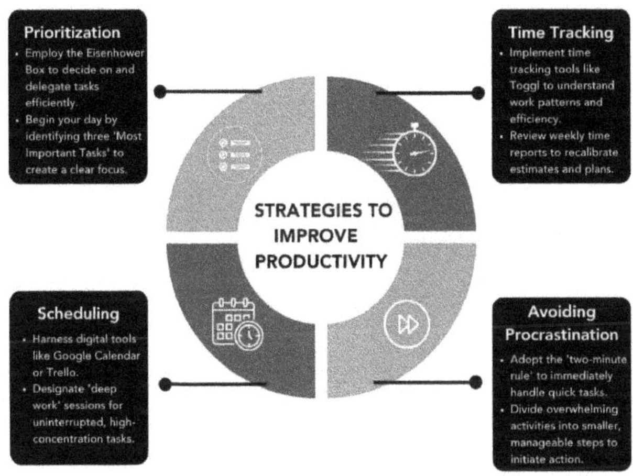

5.3 Budgeting and Cost Management

Remember the classic saying, "Look after the pennies and the pounds will look after themselves?" When it comes to project management, this tends to be true. If you've ever felt that gut-wrenching moment when you realise your project is going over budget, you're in good company. I recall a chat with a project manager who joked, "If I had a dollar for every time I've had a budget scare, I'd never need a budget again!" But budgeting jokes aside, it's a struggle many of us face. Budgets aren't just about numbers on a spreadsheet; they're the lifeblood of our projects. A healthy budget keeps everything flowing smoothly, while cost overruns can bring a project to its knees.

Let me illustrate by example. Let's say a project manager, let's call her Linda, was leading a seemingly well-planned project, but midway through, she realised she had under-budgeted for certain critical components. Panic ensued. Scrambling to find funds, she had to make some tough calls and scale back other areas of the project. It was a harrowing experience, but one that Linda swore she'd never repeat.

The Project Management Playbook

So, how do you avoid the pitfalls Linda faced? How do you ensure that your projects remain financially fit?

Here are a few ideas that I recommend you follow:

Maintain Financial Health

A project without proper financial health is like a car without fuel—it won't go far. I will show you a few strategies to keep your project's finances robust and healthy, ensuring smooth sailing from start to finish.

Avoid Cost Overruns

Unexpected expenses are the ghost stories of the project management world—scary and best avoided. I will discuss pre-emptive measures to take, ensuring that these unwelcome surprises stay far from our projects.

Ensure Profitability

At the end of the day, a project's success isn't just about completion; it's also about profitability. I will show you ways to keep your eyes on the bottom line, ensuring your projects don't just end, but end profitably.

By the end of this section, you'll be equipped with tools and strategies to make every penny work in your project's favour. Budgeting and cost management won't be daunting tasks, but rather powerful allies in your project's journey.

Aspect	Description	Examples
Realistic Budgeting	Formulate budgets that are realistic, comprehensive, and aligned with project objectives and constraints.	• Gathering historical data from past projects to estimate costs accurately. • Collaborating with team members to include all potential expenses, ensuring no hidden or unforeseen costs are left out.
Cost Monitoring	Regularly review and monitor project costs, detecting deviations early and implementing	• Using tools like Microsoft Project or QuickBooks to track project expenditures in

	corrective actions promptly.	real-time. • Setting up monthly budget review meetings to compare actual costs with projections and adjust as necessary.
Cost Optimization	Explore opportunities to optimize costs without compromising quality, such as leveraging resources efficiently and negotiating with	• Negotiating bulk purchase discounts with suppliers or exploring early payment discounts. • Assigning multi-skilled team members to various roles, reducing the need

	suppliers.	to hire additional resources.
Value Analysis	Continuously assess the value delivered by the project against the incurred costs, ensuring value maximisation.	• Using a Cost-Benefit Analysis to compare the monetary value of benefits derived from a project with the costs invested. • Surveying stakeholders post-project completion to gauge the perceived value of the project outcomes compared to the budget spent.

5.4 Stakeholder Management

We've all been there. Sitting across the table from a stakeholder who just doesn't seem to get it or trying to rally support from a group that has divergent views on where the project should head. I remember a colleague, who would Jest, "Managing the project is a breeze; it's the people that are the real puzzle!" In many ways, he wasn't wrong. People, with their varying opinions, expectations, and priorities, can be complex.

Stakeholders can make or break a project. Their influence, support, or lack thereof can determine the trajectory of your project. Think of them as the wind beneath the wings of a project. The right gust can propel us forward, while turbulence can make things... interesting.

Let's consider an example. A project manager once led a project where everything was on track. That includes timelines, budget, deliverables. But

The Project Management Playbook

he overlooked one key stakeholder who, feeling side-lined, threw a wrench into the final stages of the project. The project manager quickly realised that even the most meticulously planned project could face hurdles if stakeholders aren't managed correctly.

So, how do you ensure you are always on the right side of your stakeholders? How can you align their expectations, earn their support, and address any concerns they might have?

There are three key areas to focus on. I'll highlight them below for you.

Align All Expectations

Misaligned expectations are like setting out on a journey without a clear destination. I will show the strategies I personally use to ensure everyone's on the same page, heading in the same direction.

Garner Necessary Support

A project without stakeholder support is akin to a ship without a crew. You will learn how to get buy-in from key players, ensuring smooth sailing throughout the project's lifespan.

Address Concerns and Conflicts Early On

It's not about avoiding conflicts; it's about handling them constructively. You will tackle ways to address concerns immediately, turning potential roadblocks into advantages.

By the end of this segment, the puzzle that my colleague joked about will seem a lot less baffling. You'll be armed with the tools and insights to not just manage stakeholders, but to truly engage and collaborate with them, harnessing their strengths for the success of your project.

Aspect	Description	Examples
Stakeholder Identification	Identify all relevant stakeholders early in the project, understanding their interests, influences, and expectations.	Creating a stakeholder map to visually represent key project stakeholders and their influence or interest in the project. Conducting interviews or surveys at the outset of a project to understand stakeholder perspectives and priorities.

Stakeholder Engagement	Develop tailored engagement strategies, maintaining open and regular communication and involving stakeholders in decision-making processes.	Organising quarterly town hall meetings to update stakeholders on project progress and solicit feedback. Setting up a dedicated project communication channel or portal where stakeholders can access updates, share insights, and raise concerns.
Expectation Management	Clarify and manage stakeholder expectations realistically, addressing discrepancies and avoiding false promises.	Clearly documenting and communicating project scope, objectives, and deliverables from the beginning. Hosting expectation-setting workshops with stakeholders to ensure

		alignment and clarify project outcomes.
Conflict Resolution	Address conflicts proactively and constructively, seeking mutually beneficial solutions and maintaining harmonious relationships.	Arranging mediation sessions between conflicting parties to understand the root cause of the issue and find a middle ground. Employing a neutral third-party arbitrator for high-stake disagreements to ensure an unbiased resolution.

5.5 Frequently Asked Questions

What are some top tips for managing projects efficiently?

It starts with clear goal setting, regular communication, prioritising tasks, using the right tools, and routinely reviewing progress.

How can I manage difficult stakeholders?

There are so many types of stakeholders, yet you are likely to come across a few challenging ones along the way. I recommend taking the time to understand where they are concerned. Then creating space to communicate openly while also welcoming their feedback. Be patient and show empathy, but at times you may need to be assertive to ensure the project goes according to plan.

How often should I communicate with stakeholders?

Communication frequency varies based on the project's phase and stakeholder needs. During critical periods, it might be daily, while during more stable phases, weekly updates might be fine.

What tools can help me manage projects better?

There are numerous tools, ranging from task management apps like Trello and Asana, to more comprehensive platforms like Microsoft Project or JIRA. The best tool depends on the project's size, complexity, and specific needs. You will need to look at your project and opt for a tool that you know how to use, and can be proficient in.

What's the best way to prioritise tasks in a project?

Methods like the Eisenhower Box or the ABCD priority system can be useful. Consider factors such as task urgency, importance, dependencies, and available resources.

How can I ensure my project stays on budget?

Be sure to regularly track expenses, forecast potential costs, allocate a contingency budget, and ensure open communication with your finance team.

What should I do if my project is off-track?

This can happen often. Therefore, assess the situation, identify the root cause, and communicate with stakeholders. Then, go ahead and adjust the plan or resources as needed, and implement corrective actions.

How do I handle scope creep?

The Project Management Playbook

Clearly define the project scope from the beginning and document all changes. Once done, communicate the implications of changes, and be prepared to push back when necessary.

What are some effective strategies for stakeholder engagement?

I recommend consistent and regular updates and offering feedback sessions to keep everyone in the loop. Then involve the stakeholders in decision making when you can.

How can I build a positive relationship with stakeholders?

Be transparent, honest, and communicate often. Remember to keep promises so you can build trust and positive relationships.

5.6 Chapter Summary

The waters of project management can be tricky, filled with potential pitfalls and unexpected storms. In this chapter, you were equipped with the advice and tips I have learned on my journey of project management. Starting with communication, I like to think of it as the compass for our ship. Using great communication, you can have better conversations and give feedback in a more conducive manner. In doing so, you get better at active listening. Overall, it helps ensure everyone on board knows the course the project is charting.

In addition, time management can be thought of as your reliable crew. It helps your project stay on course and reach the destination on time. The best way to achieve good time management is through prioritisation, the balance of scheduling, and the discipline of time tracking, ensuring your project moves at optimum speed. Once you have improved your time management, you can work on budgeting and cost management. Keep an eye out on having a budget, assessing the costs regularly and ensuring every dollar spent delivers maximum value. Finally, a project without stakeholders is an impossible task. Therefore, recognize who is crucial to your project, understand their needs and ensure they are comfortable with the project process. So, align their vision, gain their trust, and tackle any issues head on.

Below is a checklist of the content covered in Chapter 5. Once you have completed each section, feel free to check them off and make notes where necessary.

Section	Action Point
The Art of Communication	Review the steps suggested to improve your communication as a project manager. Take one improvement at a time.
Time Management	Create a list of areas where your time management needs work. For example, you may decide that you need to prioritise more, then

	start focusing on this.
Budgeting and Cost Management	Review areas of your current budgeting and cost management skill set, opt for one area that needs work and work on that.
Stakeholder Management	Make a list of your key stakeholders in your recent project and rank how well you managed each relationship. Where you rated poorly, use one of the tools suggested to improve each relationship in your next project.
Reflect and Review	Reflect on the real-world applicability of each component and characteristic and review each section for thorough understanding.

In the next chapter, I share the tools of the trade. You will learn more about traditional project management tools as well as software that will make your life as a project manager simpler and more efficient.

Chapter 6: Tools of the Trade

Let's imagine project management as a massive workshop. Picture it: shelves lined with tools, some old and trusty, others shiny and new. You see, managing a project isn't too different from crafting a masterpiece in this workshop. To get the job done right, you need the right tools in hand.

Now, in this chapter, we're going to take you on a tour of our workshop. We'll dust off some of those classic, tried-and-true tools that generations of project managers have sworn by. But wait, we've also got some of the latest and greatest software solutions that tech has to offer. Whether it's for

The Project Management Playbook

keeping everyone on the same page or ensuring we're ready for any curveballs, we've got a tool for that.

By the end of this chapter, you'll know your way around this toolbox and be ready to tackle any project challenge thrown your way.

6.1 Traditional Project Management Tools

These are the traditional project management tools.

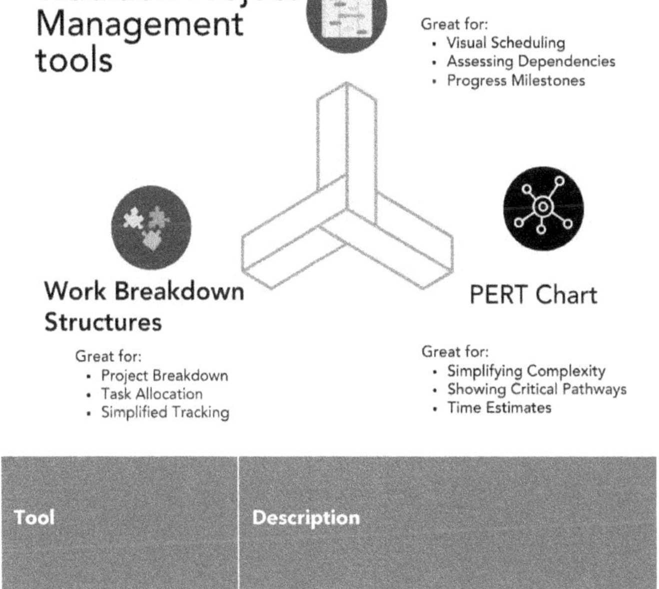

Tool	Description

Gantt Charts	A visual representation of the project schedule. It provides a clear view of task durations, dependencies, and milestones, enabling efficient time management and coordination throughout the project's life cycle.
PERT Charts	This graphical tool offers a representation of tasks and their respective timelines. It highlights the sequence of tasks and helps identify the critical path, ensuring timely completion and addressing potential bottlenecks.
Work Breakdown Structures (WBS)	A comprehensive analytical tool used to create simplified views by break downing the work into pieces that are both understandable and easy to action.

Here is a more detailed view of the tools.

The Project Management Playbook

Tool	Cool Tricks	Benefits
Gantt Charts	<ul><li>Maps out tasks that rely on others.</li><li>Highlights major wins and phases.</li><li>Assigns tasks to team members, machines, or tools.</li></ul>	<ul><li>Easily understandable.</li><li>Adaptable to changes.</li><li>Clear accountability and deadline overview.</li></ul>
PERT Charts	<ul><li>Links tasks with arrows to show project flow.</li><li>Highlights the critical path.</li><li>Offers three time estimates for every task.</li></ul>	<ul><li>Manages complex projects.</li><li>Efficient resource allocation.</li><li>Provides foresight into potential delays.</li></ul>

Work Breakdown Structures (WBS)	• Structures from broad phases to specific tasks. • Gives a visual project snapshot. • Assigns unique numbers for organisation.	• Simplifies complex projects. • Clarifies task allocation. • Facilitates easy progress tracking.

Now, let's discuss each tool and how you can use it effectively.

Gantt Charts

A Gantt chart is a horizontal bar chart used to visually represent a project schedule. For a project manager, this tool is indispensable for several reasons. The first being time management naturally. The Gantt chart allows you to set a start and end date for your individual project tasks. This is so important as it ensures that every phase of the project meets the set deadline. An example being say you are building a new software application.

For this project its tasks include the following:

- Design User Interface
- Develop Backend Functions
- Test Application

As you plot these on the Gantt chart you will see the sequence of events easily and you will also be able to spot any overlaps. In addition, you can quickly spot tasks that are running at the same time and deploy the resources needed to complete. For example, if the tasks Design interface and develop backend functionality are running at the same time, you can allocate these important tasks to separate teams. Finally, you can test progress by comparing your planned and actual progress as seen on the Gantt chart. For example, if you note that the application was meant to be tested on the 21st of this month, and preceding tasks have not been completed, then you can end up taking corrective action.

PERT Charts

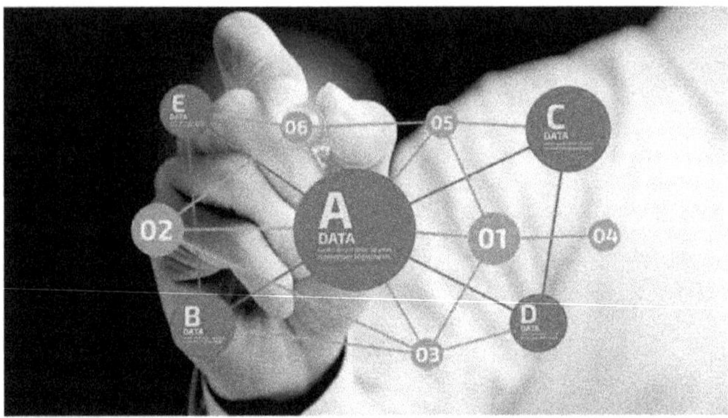

The Program Evaluation Review Technique (PERT) chart is a network diagram. It will show you the sequence of tasks and the interdependencies within the project. The sequence visualisation shows you the workflow of tasks and the order in which tasks must be completed. For example, before developing back-end functions in a software project you must first draft functional specifications. In addition, the PERT chart is effective in identifying the critical path. This means it can identify the sequence of stages and shows you the minimum time needed to complete the project. When you recognize this path, you can quickly identify delays and then allocate resources accordingly. Finally PERT charts are effective at managing risk. When you identify the slack time which is the extra time for each task, you can anticipate the delays and manage that. A good example of this is designing the logo for the new app that has a slack time of 5 days, which means this task can afford a delay of this time without affecting the next task.

Work Breakdown Structures (WBS)

Work Breakdown Structures are important because it breaks down projects into smaller more manageable tasks. Let's consider how it works next. It offers detailed planning to you where you can review the scope of a project based on sections and specific tasks. In this way, nothing gets overlooked. For example, if we are still developing a software application, the WBS would break this down into segments. These segments could be backend development, frontend development or testing. Based on these segments, more tasks could be identified to enhance specific features. This level of organisation can help you allocate teams or resources to different tasks. This will have a positive influence on the overall project. For example, if a team is good at backend development, then it may be a good idea to designate those tasks to that team and the UI or UX to a different team.

Now that you have a broad view of the traditional tools, let's take a look at modern tools in everyday use.

6.2 Project Management Software

The tools used have advanced significantly over the years. These tools I am about to share support traditional aspects of project management but also help introduce new features to improve your role as a project manager. These are the types of tools.

Project Management Software is a one stop shop for all your needs. It provides everything needed for you to have complete control of your project. The following are examples of great tools. These include JIRA, Trello, Asana, Monday.com, and Microsoft Project.

What makes these tools a standout? Firstly, they act as a taskmaster, enabling you to manage tasks, deadlines, and monitor progress of your projects. They also help with collaboration through chatting, commenting, and file sharing. One important feature is that they allow for the tracking of hours spent on tasks, ensuring efficient time management. Additionally, when it comes to detailed reports these software tools can provide all the data and graphical info needed. A great feature is that they integrate well with most other project management software too.

The Project Management Playbook

These tools are more specific, and a description is included for each below.

Tool	Description	Examples
MS Project	It's great for planning, scheduling, resource management, and tracking progress.	You can plan a project in advance. Do this by defining a project's start and end date. From here you can list out all the tasks and milestones.
		You can enhance scheduling. This is easily done by assigning specific deadlines for each task and adjusting as you need it.
		Manage resources are easily completed. This is done by allocating a budget for your project and tracking expenses. Then you can assign roles

		and responsibilities to team members.
		Track progress: The software allows you to view Gantt charts. This helps you visually track tasks progress.
Asana	This is one of the best collaboration tools. You can swiftly coordinate your team, manage tasks, and improve project visibility.	Team Coordination is done by setting up a team "workspace", inviting members, and discussing tasks in real-time.
		Manage tasks effectively by assigning tasks to team members, setting deadlines for them, and attaching needed files.
		Keep the project visible. Do this by using the project dashboard to get a high-level view of

		progress. You can quickly see what's on track and identify any roadblocks.
Trello	This is a newer tool which is more visual in nature. It uses boards and lists to organise projects and tasks. It's more intuitive.	You can create a board for a new product launch campaign.
		Within the board, make lists titled "To Do", "In Progress", and "Completed".
		Add a card for "Design Advertisements", move it from "To Do" to "In Progress" when work begins, and finally to "Completed" when done.

Jira	This is primarily an agile tool that has project management features.	Use the dashboard to review the status of various tasks, such as "To Do", "In Review", or "Done".
		Store tasks or features not currently being worked on. Prioritise them for future sprints.
		Organise tasks into two-week sprints, assign them to team members, and track their progress until completion.

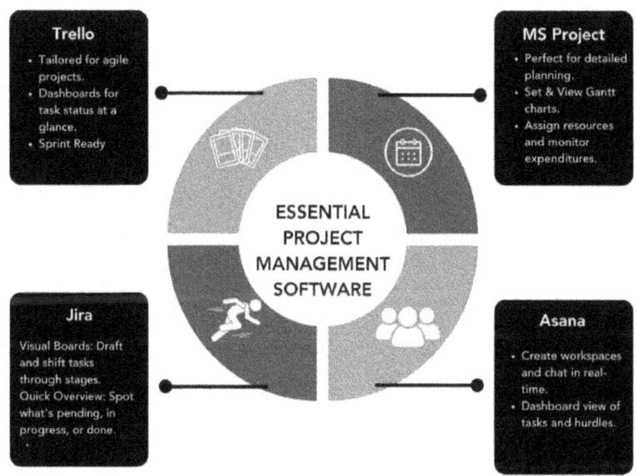

Now, let's consider the best project management communication tools.

6.3 Tools for Communication

Effective communication is a key aspect of project management. The good news is that there are many tools to help you communicate effectively. Let's consider these tools.

Tool	Features	Best Practices
Slack	They have channels for team or project-specific communication. There is direct messaging, file sharing and integration with other tools. You can have real time, organised conversations. You can also share files easily.	Create dedicated channels for specific teams and be sure to keep them organised. Link tools like Google drive, Asana, and Trello to have a better workflow. Use highlight features to quickly retrieve crucial tasks.

| **Zoom** | Zoom is ideal for HD video conferencing, screen sharing and hosting webinars. You can change the background and have break out rooms. | I recommend scheduling meetings in advance. Also share the links with participants prior.

Make use of breakout rooms especially when you have a large group. It helps to have more focussed discussions. |
| | It is quite reliable for virtual meetings. In addition, you can host large webinar sessions. You can also make your sessions interactive with screen sharing. | Record meetings and this can be saved on a shared drive for those who could not attend. |

Microsoft Teams	This is a great unified communication platform as it integrates with MS office suite allowing for great collaboration. It's so easy for you to customise with the plugins.	Just like Slack, be sure to use channels for different teams. Use tabs for pinning important documents and apps. This way your team can easily access it. Make the most of the integration with MS Office apps like Word, Excel, and PowerPoint.

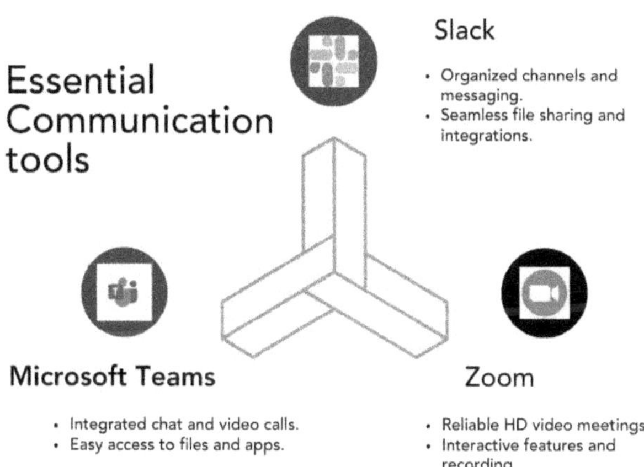

Now that you have clarity on excellent communication tools to leverage, consider risk and change management and how that can improve your project management skills.

6.4 Tools for Risk and Change Management

Managing risks and changes effectively is crucial in maintaining project stability and achieving project objectives, necessitating specialised tools designed to address these aspects.

Tool	Description	Example
Risk Register	The register is a great tool for documenting your project risks. You can show the risks identified as well as assessments and plans	A construction project many see through the risk register that a weather condition will bring delays. Since the risk is documented, then you can apply strategies like

	for mitigation.	updating schedules and purchasing protective gear.
Change Management Software	These tools help you streamline change requests, approvals, and tracking. You can control and document all changes in one place.	If a client requests a feature change for an app, the change can be quickly proposed and reviewed in one place. From there it can also show how it was approved and implemented. This enables all stakeholders to see the changes.

Impact Analysis Tools	Since changes occur you need to assess the impact on the project. Doing an impact analysis is helpful as it informs better planning and decisions too.	In the realm of product design, prior to making any change. You may leverage an impact analysis tool to see how the change will affect costs, timelines, and resources.

Now, let's consider each of the tools in more detail.

Risk Register

As we have noted, the risk register is a tool that helps you capture and document risks that may impact your project. Here is a step-by-step process to leverage the risk register:

- Identify risks by listing all potential risks that could affect your project.
- Assess the risks listed based on how likely they are to occur and have an impact on the project.
- Rank the risks you list based on their importance and significance.
- For each of the risks, note down the plan of action to manage or mitigate it.

- Monitor and review the register on a regular basis. You can do this by updating the status of risks, add new risks and document the current strategies.

Let's consider a project to launch a new website. Potential risks might include delays in content creation, technical glitches, and budget overruns. By using a Risk Register, the project team can:

- Identify: List down risks such as "Server downtime," "Content not ready," etc.
- Assess: Determine that "Server downtime" has a high impact but low likelihood.
- Prioritise: Rank "Server downtime" as a top priority risk due to its high impact.
- Mitigate: Plan for server redundancy or an alternative hosting solution.
- Monitor & Review: Regularly check server status and be prepared with a backup if needed.

Change Management Software

This type of software provides structured processes for requesting, approving, and tracking changes during a project. Here is a step-by-step process on how change management software can be used effectively:

- Stakeholders or submit change requests highlighting the nature and reasons for the proposed change.
- You or designated teams review the request, evaluating its feasibility, impact, and necessity.
- Based on the assessment, changes are approved or declined.

The Project Management Playbook

- Approved changes are communicated and implemented.
- The software tracks the status of the change, from request to completion.

Let's consider an example of an IT project. If a client requests a new feature addition to an application. With Change Management Software:

- Request: The client submits a detailed feature request.
- Assess: The development team evaluates the feasibility and impact on the project timeline.
- Approve: The project manager approves the change after considering its benefits and implications.
- Implement: Developers add the new feature.
- Track: The software tracks the feature development progress until its completion.

Impact Analysis Tools

These tools look at the overall consequences of changes on different parts of the project. Here is a step-by-step process on how it works:

- You can start by feeding the tool with current project data and the proposed change details.
- The tool evaluates the change's potential effects on time, costs, resources, and other critical project parameters.
- The tool generates a report detailing the expected impacts of the change.
- Project managers use the report to make informed decisions about whether to proceed with the change.

The Project Management Playbook

For example, in a manufacturing project, a proposal is made to use a different material. Using an Impact Analysis Tool:

- Input: Data about the current material and proposed material is entered.
- Analysis: The tool assesses how the new material might affect production speed, costs, product quality, etc.
- Report: The report indicates the new material could increase costs but enhance product durability.
- Decision-making: The management decides to proceed with the change, deeming the enhanced product durability a worthy trade-off for the increased cost.

6.5 Frequently asked questions

What are some essential tools every project manager should know?

The Project Management Playbook

Tools like JIRA, Trello, Asana, Microsoft Project, and Monday.com are widely recognized for project management. Version control systems like Git, and CI/CD tools such as Jenkins are also important in tech-related projects.

How do I choose the right project management software (PMS) for my team?

Consider factors such as the project's size, the team's familiarity with tools, integration capabilities, scalability, and budget constraints. You can opt for trial versions to test the tool's fit.

What's the significance of version control systems in software projects?

Version control systems track changes to the codebase, allow multiple developers to work concurrently, manage conflicts, and provide a history of code changes, ensuring smooth collaboration and security.

How do CI/CD tools enhance project efficiency?

Continuous Integration and Continuous Deployment tools automate testing and deployment processes, ensuring that new code integrations don't introduce errors, thereby speeding up software development and enhancing code quality.

Are traditional project management tools obsolete with the advent of newer digital solutions? Not necessarily. While digital solutions offer advanced features, traditional tools like Gantt charts remain effective for visualising project timelines and dependencies.

How do tools aid in stakeholder communication and collaboration?

The Project Management Playbook

Modern PMS often comes with integrated chat, comments, file-sharing features, and reporting modules. These facilitate real-time collaboration, information sharing, and transparency with stakeholders.

Is there a steep learning curve associated with these tools?

The learning curve varies. Some tools are user-friendly with intuitive interfaces, while others might require training. Organisations often provide tutorials, workshops, or onboarding sessions for smoother transitions.

Can one tool suffice for all project management needs?

While some comprehensive tools offer a suite of functionalities, often a combination of specialised tools yields the best results, especially for large or complex projects.

How do I ensure the security and privacy of project data while using these tools?

Choose tools with robust security features, conduct regular security audits, restrict access based on roles, and train team members on security best practices.

Are there industry-specific project management tools?

Yes, certain tools cater to specific industries, like construction, healthcare, or software development, offering specialised features relevant to the respective domain.

6.6 Chapter Summary

In Chapter 6, I shared the essential tools needed to work effectively as a project manager. There were the tried and tested tools such as Gantt Charts, PERT charts and WBS. Each of these tools offer unique views of how your project is progress. Additionally, you looked at modern software tools such as MS Project, Asana, Trello, and Jira, and their transformative impact on project coordination, tracking, and communication. Not stopping there, we then navigated the significance of communication tools, emphasising the pivotal roles of Slack, Zoom, and Microsoft Teams in fostering seamless team interactions. I also showed you how to leverage the power of the Risk Register, Change Management Software, and Impact Analysis Tools. Below is a summary of the content covered in Chapter 6. As you journey through each section, feel free to mark your progress and jot down your insights for future reference.

Section	Action Point
Traditional Project Management Tools	Familiarise yourself with Gantt Charts, PERT Charts, and SWOT Analysis. Consider how they can be incorporated into your current or upcoming projects.

Modern Project Management Software	Assess the features of MS Project, Asana, Trello, and Jira. Reflect on which tool(s) best suit your project's needs and team dynamics.
Communication Tools	Evaluate the communication dynamics of your team. Contemplate the integration of Slack, Zoom, or Microsoft Teams to enhance collaborative efforts.
Risk and Change Management Tools	Dive deep into the Risk Register, Change Management Software, and Impact Analysis Tools. Consider how to implement them to anticipate and manage project risks and changes.
Case Study	Analyse the case studies provided for each tool. What practical insights can you gather and implement in your projects?

Reflect and Review	Reflect on the versatility and applicability of each tool. Review each section to ensure a comprehensive grasp and consider their integration in your project management journey.

As Chapter 6 ends you now have knowledge of tools that can enhance your project management skills, from traditional tools to risk and change management. These tools not only make the project management process more efficient but also ensure that every stakeholder is on the same page.

However, understanding the tools is not enough. In the next chapter, "Final Thoughts and the Road Ahead", we will reflect upon and summarise the key insights from all the preceding chapters. Furthermore, Chapter 7 will offer invaluable tips to aid in the practical application of these insights, ensuring you're well-prepared to navigate the challenges and opportunities in your project management journey.

Chapter 7: Final Thoughts & Road Ahead

In my early days as a project manager, I was leading a software development project that seemed to be progressing smoothly. However, halfway through, we were hit with the news of a major industry regulation change. This unexpected twist meant our software, once completed, would no longer be compliant. Instead of panicking, our team held a brainstorming session. We soon pivoted, integrating the necessary changes. We managed to deliver the project on time. This experience taught me the invaluable lesson of adaptability and the importance of having a team ready to face unforeseen challenges. The significance of being ready for changes cannot be overstated.

As projects become more complex and cross-functional, the ability to anticipate changes effectively, support team members and stakeholders, and communicate becomes crucial. A successful project manager isn't just someone who knows the ins and outs of a Gantt chart but someone who can navigate the intricacies of change, foster a positive team environment, and lead with assuredness.

With that being said, it is now time to wrap up our journey together learning about project management. It's been an exhilarating journey, hasn't it? From the foundations we've built to the strategies we've adopted; project management is so much more than just a set of tools. It is a philosophy, a discipline, and, for many, a passion. Over the course of this book, I have shown you the rich tapestry of the history of project management, the current state and how you can best leverage the tools and tricks to become a better project manager. Now, let's set our sights on the future of project management and how that impacts you. As you try to keep up with technological revolutions and the rise of the digital age, and using tools like Asana, Jira and Microsoft Project while employing Agile methodologies to deliver projects, you should also think about what's on the horizon. The future is in place for AI, big data analytics, and cloud computing. These are no longer just buzzwords, but vital components of our toolkit. The shift isn't just about tech, though. The modern project manager is becoming an emotional intelligence expert, a collaboration maestro, and a cross-functional leader.

Essentially, your journey learning about project management has taken you from learning, to applying and now contemplating the vision of the future. Your future as a project manager.

So, what's next? It seems evident that project management is not simply evolving but it is revolutionising. Let us consider this revolution.

7.1 The Ever-evolving Nature of Project Management

In the early 2000s, project managers were heavily relying on chunky binders, overflowing with spreadsheets, and whiteboards littered with sticky notes. Now, fast-forward to today, and those binders have been replaced by sleek software applications, and whiteboards have gone digital.

That's the dynamic world of project management for you! Just as smartphones evolved from rotary phones and streaming platforms emerged from VHS tapes, project management too has seen its own series of transformations. With every shift in technology, societal needs, or even global events, project management has danced to the rhythm, reshaping its methods and tools.

In this section, we'll dive into the fascinating journey of how project management keeps reinventing itself. This will help you determine what to do in the next phase of your project management career.

Aspect	Description	Example
Adapt	This is an ongoing adjustment of project management methodologies to fit the ever-changing business world and shifts in technology.	The shift from traditional Waterfall methodologies to Agile practices in software development.

Integrate	As technology continues to advance, project management integrates these advancements. This improves processes, communication, and overall efficiency.	The adoption of AI-driven tools to forecast project risks or VR tools for remote team meetings.
Diversify	As various sectors recognize the importance of project management, unique tools and methods are developed to cater to these specific industry requirements.	The emergence of construction project management tools for construction-specific needs or healthcare project management focusing on patient care and hospital infrastructure.

Here are a few examples of the changing nature of project management in different industries.

Nokia's Shift from Mobile Phones to Network Infrastructure

The Project Management Playbook

Once the world's largest supplier of mobile phones, Nokia faced a sharp decline with the rise of smartphones. But rather than fading into obscurity, Nokia pivoted. They recognized the need to adapt and shifted their primary focus to network infrastructure, subsequently acquiring Alcatel-Lucent, a global telecom equipment company. This strategic move was not just a business pivot; it was a massive project management challenge, involving the integration of technologies, teams, and corporate cultures. Nokia's journey underscores the importance of adaptability in project management, especially in a rapidly changing business landscape.

Walmart's Integration of Blockchain for Food Safety

With the growing demand for transparency in the supply chain, especially in food products, Walmart turned to blockchain technology. The retail giant collaborated with IBM to develop a blockchain-based system that could trace the origin of produce within seconds, a process that previously took days. This project's success was not merely about leveraging new tech but also about managing multiple stakeholders, from farmers to store managers, ensuring that the system was both robust and user-friendly. It's an excellent example of how modern project management isn't just about timelines and resources but integrating novel technologies for tangible business outcomes.

SpaceX's Starlink Project

SpaceX's ambition to provide global internet coverage through its Starlink satellite constellation is an example of specialised project management. Given the aerospace industry's complexities, the project demands unique risk assessments, coordination with international space agencies, and multiple logistical challenges. SpaceX's iterative launch strategy, constant technological improvements to its satellite design, and active stakeholder management underscore the importance of specialised project management approaches tailored to specific industry needs.

7.2 Staying Updated with Industry Trends

As a project manager, you must constantly read the tides and changes within the industry.

If you wait too long, you might find yourself off-course, battling unexpected storms. Therefore, recognizing the early signs of changing trends is a key to your success.

Being in the know isn't just about looking modern or speaking the latest industry jargon. It's about embracing a forward-thinking mindset. This means not just navigating through today's challenges, but also setting the sails for tomorrow's horizons. It's about predicting potential pitfalls, harnessing innovative tools and methodologies, and ensuring that every project decision aligns with the broader industry landscape.

Throughout history, the most impactful leaders and organisations have been those that didn't merely react to change but anticipated and shaped it.

The Project Management Playbook

The purpose of this section is to show you how to keep your finger on the pulse of the industry, ensuring you're not just keeping up, but truly leading the way. Here are three key steps you can take to be impactful as a project manager.

Steps	Action Point
Keep learning and developing skills	<ul><li>Embrace opportunities for skill enhancement.</li><li>Consider online courses, workshops, and seminars related to the latest trends in project management.</li><li>Reflect on the practical applications of what you learn and how you can integrate them into your current projects.</li></ul>
Participate in Professional Communities	<ul><li>Join reputed project management forums</li><li>Attend local PMI chapter meetings or engage in online discussions related to project management.</li><li>Share your experiences, ask</li></ul>

	questions, and collaborate with peers to gain a diverse perspective on the industry's evolution.
Proactively Explore Emerging Trends	• Dedicate time regularly to research and read about the latest innovations, tools, and methodologies in project management. • Think about how you can implement these trends in your projects or how they might influence the future of your work.

Below, I've included three examples of opportunities within the project management field to take note of.

The Agile Revolution

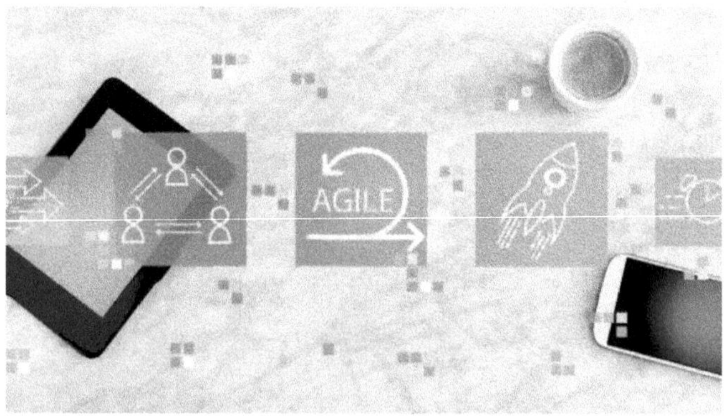

A few decades ago, the Waterfall methodology was the dominant approach in software development projects. However, with the IT industry's rapid evolution, project managers found this method to be restrictive. Enter Agile. This is more a flexible and collaborative approach to project management that changed the industry. The shift wasn't merely about a new method; it showed the importance of continuous learning. Project managers who quickly adopted and mastered Agile methodologies had a distinct advantage. This is important for you as new methodologies make their way into project management you must stay updated and be adaptive to the changes.

The Role of PMI (Project Management Institute) in Professional Development

PMI, a global community of project professionals, has played a pivotal role in standardising project management practices across the world. By participating in PMI, many project managers have not only expanded their knowledge base but also networked with industry peers, sharing challenges and solutions. Regular events, workshops, and seminars by PMI and similar organisations offer platforms for project managers to stay informed about industry benchmarks, best practices, and emerging trends.

The Project Management Playbook

This is another area where you can keep expanding your knowledge and experience.

Incorporating AI in Project Forecasting

Artificial Intelligence (AI) has been a game-changer in many industries. This is also true for project management. Companies that proactively explored the potential of AI found incredible applications, one of which is project forecasting. By analysing vast amounts of data from past projects, AI tools can predict potential risks, recommend resource allocations, and even suggest optimal timelines. A proactive exploration of this trend allowed several enterprises to benefit. In this way, you can leverage the power of AI to mitigate risks, optimise costs, and streamline project executions.

7.3 The Next Generation of Project Managers

Project management is in a perpetual relay, with seasoned professionals ready to hand over the baton to a fresh wave of project leaders. These upcoming project managers are stepping into an arena marked by intricate projects, state-of-the-art tools, and sky-high expectations. While this may seem daunting, it's also ripe with so many brilliant opportunities. In this way, when you learn from the experience shared within this book, you are also benefiting from the opportunity to expand your skills and enhance your career.

As you look ahead, remember your role transcends managing projects. It's about being mentors and champions for those who will shape the future of this dynamic discipline. Through guidance, resources, and a sprinkle of inspiration, you can be part of an ever-changing story of project management. Here are a few opportunities to take advantage of.

Opportunities	Action Point
Mentorship and Guidance	<ul><li>If you are an experienced project manager, consider offering mentorship to newcomers in the field.</li><li>Share anecdotes, challenges faced, and the strategies you've employed over the years.</li><li>Encourage the mentees to ask questions and seek guidance regularly.</li></ul>
Educational Outreach and Opportunities	<ul><li>Partner with educational institutions or organisations to provide workshops, seminars, or guest lectures about project management.</li><li>Explore creating or supporting scholarship programs for project management courses.</li></ul>

Inspiration and Empowerment	<ul><li>Share success stories, innovative projects, and breakthrough moments in your project management journey to inspire others.</li><li>Encourage creativity and new ideas, emphasising that every project manager has the potential to bring something unique to the table.</li></ul>

7.4 Frequently Asked Questions

Why is it important to reflect on the evolution of project management?

Reflecting on its evolution helps us appreciate the adaptability and resilience of the discipline. Understanding past challenges and successes can guide future practices and decisions.

How does staying updated with industry trends benefit project managers?

Being updated allows project managers to anticipate challenges. They can leverage modern tools and techniques, align strategies with industry shifts, and ensure their teams remain competitive and efficient.

What role will technology play in the future of project management?

Technology will continue to introduce advanced tools, automation, data analytics, and AI-driven insights. This will lead to more efficient project execution and stakeholder management.

How can we inspire the next generation of project managers?

Through mentorship programs, educational outreach, seminars. Additionally, providing them with resources and platforms to learn, innovate, and lead.

With project complexities increasing, how can future project managers prepare?

Embracing continuous learning, upskilling, staying abreast of industry trends, and cultivating a mindset of adaptability will be key.

What's the importance of soft skills in the future of project management?

The Project Management Playbook

As projects become more interdisciplinary and stakeholder-centric, soft skills like communication, empathy, and leadership will be as crucial as technical expertise.

Are traditional project management methodologies still relevant?

While modern methodologies gain traction, traditional methodologies still offer valuable frameworks, especially for projects that have a well-defined scope and predictable variables.

How can organisations support the growth and evolution of project management?

Investing in training, tools, research, and creating a culture that values innovation, feedback, and continuous improvement can propel the discipline forward.

Will AI and automation replace the role of a project manager?

While AI and automation will handle repetitive tasks and offer insights, the human touch in decision-making, relationship management, and strategic planning remains irreplaceable. They will augment, not replace, the role.

The essence is that project management, as a discipline, is ever evolving. Embracing change, continuous learning, and preparing the next generation are pivotal to its future success and relevance.

Now that you have a deeper understanding of what it takes to be a great project manager, you can swiftly start applying the knowledge you have learned. I have also created a list of great resources and books for you to reference in the appendix section. These resources when used in conjunction with this book will continue to enhance your project management skills.

Thank you for spending the time growing your skills as a project manager. I wish you all the best on your journey ahead.

Appendix

A.1: Glossary of Common Project Management Terms

Project

A temporary endeavour undertaken to create a unique product, service, or result.

Stakeholder

An individual, group, or organisation that may affect, be affected by, or perceive itself to be affected by a decision, activity, or outcome of a project.

Scope

The sum of the products, services, and results to be provided as a project.

Risk

An uncertain event or condition that, if it occurs, has a positive or negative effect on one or more project objectives.

Baseline

The approved version of a work product that can be changed only through formal change control procedures.

Gantt Chart

A bar chart representing a schedule of tasks over time.

PERT Chart

The Project Management Playbook

A graphical representation of a project's schedule, showing the sequence of tasks and the critical path.

Agile

A project management and product development approach that prioritises flexibility and customer satisfaction.

Waterfall Model

A linear-sequential life cycle model where each phase must be completed before the next one begins.

A.2: Additional Resources and Reading Recommendations

Books

- "A Guide to the Project Management Body of Knowledge (PMBOK Guide)" by PMI: A comprehensive guide providing a standardised set of project management practices and knowledge areas.
- "The Lean Startup" by Eric Ries: A seminal book offering insights into innovative project management and product development strategies focusing on startups.
- "Scrum: The Art of Doing Twice the Work in Half the Time" by Jeff Sutherland: An essential read for those interested in the Scrum methodology and its applications in project management.

The Project Management Playbook

Websites

Project Management Institute (PMI)

The world's leading association for project management, offering certifications, resources, and a community for project managers.

Scrum Alliance

A professional organisation that provides resources, training, and support for Scrum practitioners.

Online Courses

Coursera Project Management Specialization

A series of courses providing comprehensive knowledge and skills in project management.

LinkedIn Learning

Offers a variety of courses in project management across different methodologies and tools